CARL MYDANS, PHOTOJOURNALIST

CARL MYDANS,
PHOTOJOURNALIST

BY CARL MYDANS

WITH AN INTERVIEW BY PHILIP B. KUNHARDT, JR.

HARRY N. ABRAMS, INC., PUBLISHERS

CONTENTS

Project Director: Margaret L. Kaplan
Designer: Bob McKee
Editorial Assistant: Margaret Rennolds

Library of Congress Cataloging in Publication Data
Mydans, Carl.
   Carl Mydans, photojournalist.
   1. Photography, Journalistic.   2. Mydans, Carl.
I. Title.
TR820.M93   1985   779.990982   84-24349
ISBN 0-8109-1323-2

Text copyright © 1985 Carl Mydans

Interview copyright © 1985 by Philip B. Kunhardt, Jr.

Published in 1985 by Harry N. Abrams, Incorporated, New York
A Times Mirror Company

Printed in Japan

CARL MYDANS, PHOTOJOURNALIST

From my earliest years I have been fascinated by human behavior. By the time I used a camera seriously I had become an obsessive people-watcher, observing mannerisms and body postures, the slants and curves of mouths, the falseness of smiles, the directness or evasion of eyes. When I learned to understand these signals and interpret them, I had found a source of stories as wide and as varied and as captivating as the human race.

I wanted to tell these stories, and because I was a photographer I became a storyteller in pictures. And as such a narrator with a camera in the early 1930s, I entered into the most significant revolution in communications since the invention of the printing press.

Photography is more than a hundred years old, but not until my professional lifetime has storytelling with a camera become a major form of reporting. In fact, the revolution it created is so recent that some of the photographers who pioneered the breakthrough in picture journalism, which first appeared in the U.S. in *LIFE* magazine in 1936, are still taking pictures for publication today.

Today the camera provides as much information to the world as the written word. And since there are no language barriers, it may be mankind's most important means of communication. Today, little happens in the world that is not reported in pictures as well as in words, and in many cases the photographic coverage has a far more powerful and lasting impact.

The photographer who covers news stories—or finds his stories in the lives of ordinary people as well as in world history—is a photojournalist. By training and experience, he or she becomes attuned to the movement of events and develops a sense of what is coming.

Carl Mydans during the battle for Manila, February 1945.

When *LIFE* was born, the photojournalist had not yet sprung clear of the old stereotype of the press photographer who wore a fedora hat with a press card sticking in it and worked with a 4 x 5 Speed Graphic to which was affixed a flashgun and a reflector pan. All his pictures of people and groups were the same: flashlighted with the identical intensity and fixed exposure of a single bulb, which produced unvarying overlighted foregrounds falling off immediately to backgrounds black as tunnels. He was often depicted in Hollywood as a cynical, wisecracking "bang-box boy" committed to following a glamorous and masterful reporter and awaiting the command: "Shoot that."

This image changed dramatically after the editors of *LIFE* chose a different kind of photographer to cover the news. Most of them used the 35mm camera and generally relied on available light. There was depth and a sense of action caught in their photographs that gave excitement to the pages of *LIFE*. Many editors across the country, watching what was happening at *LIFE*, called its growing staff "the new breed."

And the editors of *LIFE*, understanding where their strength lay, made their photographers princes and sent them out with researchers and reporters to smooth their way. Their work became so popular that *LIFE*'s telephones rang steadily with invitations to the photographers to functions in homes and schools and factories and often events concocted just to get them there. Soon it began to appear as though nothing ever happened without the presence of a *LIFE* photographer.

The New Yorker captured this in a memorable cartoon. It showed a bride and groom in their bridal suite, the bride just taking off her veil, as three young men with cameras enter the room. The caption reads, "But we're from *LIFE*!"

Today many reporters of the printed word carry cameras too, and some do very well with them. And they should, for both the journalist in text and the photojournalist are after a story, and what they are looking for, and the way they get it, may not be all that different. An experience I once had with Admiral Hyman Rickover might illustrate this.

In 1958 the U.S.S. *Nautilus,* the world's first nuclear submarine, became the first vessel ever to pass under the polar ice cap. During a scheduled visit to New York in August of that year Admiral Rickover was to be honored as the father of nuclear submarines.

I was sent to cover Rickover and, along with a great many other reporters and photographers, accompanied him aboard the *Nautilus* and attended his receptions at City Hall and the Brooklyn Navy Yard. I had never met the admiral, and in the crush of the coverage was not formally introduced. But sometime during the lull in the activities he came over to me and said, "What are you taking all these pictures for?"

I told him that I was covering his visit for *LIFE* magazine. He replied crisply that he knew all that. "But why are you taking so many pictures? *LIFE* can use only a few, and you've been taking them steadily all day."

"That's right," I said. "But what I'm doing is not so exceptional. You've been followed by a lot of reporters, too, and they've been scribbling notes all day as steadily as I've been taking pictures. They can't use all the things they've written down. What will happen to them is that by the time they get back to their offices they will have decided on a story line, and they'll shuffle through their notebooks, flipping over page after page to find the scenes and color and quotes that will make their story. And somewhere along the way as I take your picture, I'll see a story line too. That is, among the pictures that I've taken, or may yet take today, I shall find pictures that best tell the story of your visit. And I shall go through the contact prints of everything I've taken—very nearly as quickly as a writer selects from his notes—and mark the frames to be printed. And it's from these prints that the editors will make the choice for a story that will appear next week."

Admiral Rickover listened carefully and then said with a small smile, "Thank you for your good answer."

Most photographers remember very nearly every picture they have taken. Some, who like myself have made perhaps half a million, may remember all of them. And if a picture of theirs appears somewhere later, over the years, they will spot it immediately and, like a parent unexpectedly seeing the face of a son or daughter in a crowd, may hold it in view for a moment with the feeling that it is something profoundly theirs. In fact, they may even recognize some pictures as their own that they have never seen, because photojournalists in the field often ship their film to their home offices unprocessed and do not have a chance to see those pictures that are not published. Their editors, always pressed for time, have creamed off what they think is the best of the take and sent the rest to the files where they may languish for years.

Still, during that instant of seeing the subject through the viewfinder there is a remarkable imprinting on his memory. Once a photographer sees and captures an image through his camera it becomes his for his lifetime. And he remembers not only the picture and the circumstances of his getting it, but his feelings when he pressed the shutter.

When I look at the picture of the execution of Police Chief Pietro Caruso, the Questore of Rome, in 1944, the entire experience flashes before me: the scene, the smells, the sounds, and especially my own feelings and reactions as I stood witness with my cameras.

It was such a grave experience, and I was so unnerved by the volley that followed the photograph on page 98, that the picture of the actual shooting was blurred and unusable. And in another picture I made that year, in Grenoble, of the shooting of six young Frenchmen accused of collaboration with the Germans, the movement of my camera again blurred the picture (page 107), demonstrating an inner force that rebelled against my photographing the scene that I was witnessing.

But the world is not made up entirely of violence and disaster. And not all photographs a photojournalist makes are of unpleasant events. The picture of Vice-President John Nance Garner published here carries me back to a surprisingly pleasant experience, although I never made the picture that might have delighted my editors.

In 1939 *LIFE* decided to do a story on the closing of Congress and I was sent to Washington to photograph a number of congressmen. It was a story with an early deadline and I was young and inexperienced in Washington. And I was having trouble rounding up as many congressmen as we needed. Finally, on a tip, I learned that a number of them were closeted with the vice-president in his office, preparing for the closing session that night.

I sent in a note and Garner invited me to photograph the gathering, which was a break for me and a considerable gesture on the part of the vice-president, because in the past few days he had been under heavy attack by the labor leader John L. Lewis, who denounced him as "a poker-playing, whiskey-drinking, evil old man." And the headline writers loved it and spread it across the country. He didn't need more publicity just then.

I took a number of portraits of the various congressmen gathered there. And when the meeting was ending the vice-president raised his voice: "Well, it's time we all had a drink." And to his young male secretary: "Let's have some whiskey and branch water." There was a lot of light talk as the first drink was poured for Garner himself and he sat holding it while the other glasses were filled. Then, as he raised his glass to drink, he saw me. My cameras were hanging on my chest and my hands were by my sides, but perhaps he thought he saw them twitching.

He leaned forward and, holding his glass slightly toward me as the voices in the room fell quiet, said, "You wouldn't, would you?"

"No sir!" I exclaimed, my voice catching a little, perhaps because of my guilty thoughts. The room broke into laughter.

For the rest of the time I stood in a corner with my hands by my sides, and when the congressmen drifted out I started out too. But Garner stopped me. "Well, son," he said, "you've got a job to do, so let's do it." And while his secretary rushed to clear away the bottle and glasses, the vice-president sat in a cane rocking chair, holding his cigar just so and crossing his legs, his high laced shoes glistening, marking an era long past on the congressional scene.

When I finished he walked me to the door and put his arm around my shoulder. "I hope you got some good ones, son," he said. I did. But the one that remains in my mind is the one I didn't take.

I have spent a good part of my life being wishful about the lives that others live, and I often have a craving to be a participant in the stories that I cover. The stereotype of the reporter as an aloof observer can seldom be applied to me; I care too deeply about the people and the places that I cover. And when I look through the pictures that have been gathered for this book, I feel again the pull of that desire to be involved.

When I covered a cattle drive from Mexico to Texas in 1937, riding herd beside the vaqueros day after day, I soon identified with them so intensely I could think of no better life than to be a cowhand riding the range. And later, when I photographed the building of the tunnel under the East River in New York City, I so admired the sandhogs who worked under high air pressure in the muck that I wanted to be like them.

I became so involved in the elopement of the daughter of Antenor Patiño, "the Bolivian tin king," in London in 1954 that when the irate father tried to ferret them out and stop the marriage with his millions, I not only got into their hideout to photograph them, but found my sympathy leading me into bringing them food and becoming the conduit to the minister who agreed to marry them.

And once I got so carried away by the story told me by a fifteen-year-old boy at the Springhill mine disaster in Nova Scotia in 1958 that I began to weave the major part of my coverage around him. He had come up to me as I was photographing the anxious relatives waiting for word at the pithead.

"Whatcha takin pichers of?" he asked.

"The families whose men are caught down there in the mine," I told him.

We looked at each other a moment. I was reluctant to ask him, but at last I said, "Have you got someone down there?"

He nodded.

"Who?"

"My father and my brother."

Carl Mydans and George Silk, two LIFE combat photographers, meet during the battles for Rome, June 1944.

Carl Mydans and David Douglas Duncan in 1950, during their coverage of the Korean War.

"Where's your mother?"

"She's in the hospital. She's got hysterics."

As I photographed him the thought began to grow that I might make him the centerpiece of my story. Perhaps he could serve as the dramatic representative of all those wives and children of trapped miners who have waited and prayed at pitheads over the years.

I took him home, just down the road, and photographed him in front of his house, a clapboard shack like the other miners' homes. Then I went over the hasty notes I had made and in asking more questions learned that it was not a single brother down there with his father, it was two!

A man came out of the house and went into the nearby privy. I caught up with him when he came out and pointed at the boy who had gone on and was disappearing down the weed-edged road. "Do you know anything about that boy?" I asked.

"Sure," the man said. "He's my son."

"Your son! He told me that you were down in the mine, caught there yesterday with the others. You and your two other sons."

"No, I wasn't on that shift," he answered. "And I only got one other son and he's a boxer." He shook his head. "That boy's always imagining things."

I never saw the boy again, and I scrapped the captions on him. But my notebook is still rich with the things he said to me. And the image of his face that my camera caught, the interest that he kindled, are still there in my memory.

I did not set out to choose the pictures for this book because they had people in them but rather because they caught the drama and the history that I was witnessing. But it turned out when I made my final selection that only six out of all the photographs included here do not show people. And even in such pictures as the bombing of Chungking on page 73, it is the people—invisible as they are—whose implied presence often makes the photograph more powerful. Because we are human we see, or imagine we see, people everywhere. In the universality of our humanity we are there. And the more dramatic or more threatening the surroundings, the more deeply we feel about the people involved.

In the great majority of the pictures in this book it is the human image and the drama of human behavior that have caught the storyteller. Look at the picture at the top of page 104 of a French woman whose head is being shaved. She had given herself to the hated Germans during those months of occupation. And now the Germans have been driven out, and in the first hours of liberation she has been caught—that's the word—as she tried to flee from the villagers who chased her like a rabbit. Now, in shame, she is being shaved as a public symbol of her disgrace. But note also those leering, jeering, laughing faces behind her. What is more shameful than human beings enjoying the pain of others?

Or see the German soldier on page 97 with his arms raised. He has just been taken in a vicious firefight south of Rome. Look in his eyes and see his fright. The moment of capture in battle is a terrible moment. There is always the searing question, Are they going to kill me? He doesn't know. Watching him through the finder, I don't know either. At this moment his stomach is churning, and mine churns too. Sometimes I increase the speed of my shutter because my hands are shaking so.

Very nearly every person I have photographed is as permanently engraved on my memory as his image is on my film. Some come back in quick flashes, others in extensive vignettes. The fishlike coldness of Clark Gable and Carole Lombard's glamour as they performed on cue before a crowd of fans at a Hollywood preview in 1936 (page 204) gave me a quick insight into the movie industry of that era.

On the other hand, the warmth and humanity of Gertrude Stein and Alice B. Toklas bring back a string of memories. The picture on page 204 was taken in September, 1944, when a group of American war correspondents led by Eric Sevareid liberated them in a little village in southern France as the Germans were retreating. They had lived in hiding during the whole occupation, their secret tenaciously kept by everyone in the village for nearly four years.

Alice Toklas baked a cake and Gertrude Stein stuck an American flag in it to celebrate. To me they were a symbol of strength, living as they had under constant fear of discovery and with German officers frequently occupying the very household where they lived. "Gertrude wrote every day, secretly," her friend told me with pride. And before we left, the author scribbled a note to me which reads, "We have no more wishes because anything we wish is as we wish and though we are wishes always." She signed it and below her signature wrote, "And yet we wish well of course we wish."

I have taken many portraits, and each one has been a unique experience of communication with my subject. I had been told that William Faulkner did not like to have his picture taken, but he gave me a gentle, low-voice welcome when I came into the room: "How good of you to come all this way to take my picture," he said. And several times as I was photographing him he asked, "Please tell me if this is right for you. I want to give you what you need." Perhaps my liking and admiration for this man of genius came through in the photograph on page 199.

The meeting I had with Ezra Pound in Italy in June of 1940 underscores the differences in human behavior. He was living in Milan and broadcasting frequently for Mussolini and the cause of Fascism.

Although we were not yet in the war, many Americans considered him a traitor for his bitter attacks on the Allies and his blatant anti-Semitism. The day I found him he was willing to talk but adamant against my taking any pictures of him. But after a long lunch during which he spoke for hours while I took notes, he caught me off guard as we were saying good-bye at the restaurant door. "Well," he said, putting on his Western sombrero and adjusting the brim, "where do you want me?" (page 193).

Some people are impatient with photographers and often rude. Winston Churchill said he abhorred them, and his disdain shows in the pictures I made of him over the years, like the one on page 207. "They sound like a chorus singing 'One more. One more. One more,'" he once grumbled to me. But there are others who have an inner dignity and patience. I remember the lovely face and the courage of a young Vietnamese woman (on page 179) who sat with her head high when I photographed her in Saigon during the Tet offensive in 1968. Her home had burned and many of her family were missing, but she did not grumble.

Perhaps one reason some people are reluctant to have their picture taken is their fear that the photographer will see more than they would like to show. When I first photographed Henry Kissinger (page 206) he was thirty-five years old and still relatively unknown outside the student-faculty group at Harvard, where he lectured on international studies. But he was to have a book published on world strategy, and I was sent to photograph him in New York on the first day of 1958. I found him an interesting subject but did not see hints of greatness in his face, and in my notebook I wrote at the time: "Young, genial European intellectual with a German accent. All his fingernails are bitten to the quick so that his fingers end in stubby red lumps. But he seems calm enough on the surface and was helpful and agreeable."

Personal contacts and friendships are important to any journalist but even more so for the photojournalist, because when one is reporting in pictures one must be on the scene physically. There is no opportunity to be filled in later after an event is over. And there is no way to photograph an action secondhand. Good contacts are therefore very valuable, especially in covering wars.

Both officers and men in combat zones appreciate the presence of reporters and photographers who have shared their experiences and dangers, and they often give them special consideration in later operations. Frequently true comradeship is forged in combat, though occasionally the connection may be more a matter of public relations. General Mark Clark, commander of the Fifth Army in the Italian campaign, not only had army photographers attached to his command whose sole mission was to photograph him, but he was especially available to photojournalists who came through his headquarters.

Late in the Italian campaign, when the combined U.S.-French invasion of southern France was imminent, I decided to cover the landing at Saint-Tropez with a French division, the Third DIA under General Joseph de Goislard de Monsabert. I had been with his troops during the fight to take Siena and the general was a man I liked very much. But soon after the invasion force left the Italian coast for France, I received orders from General de Lattre de Tassigny, Commander-in-Chief of the French invasion force, to come aboard his ship, the S.S. *Battory*.

After a day's confusion and delay, a boat was sent to take me from General Monsabert's ship to the *Battory*, where de Lattre greeted me in a rage: "Yesterday I gave orders for you to come aboard this ship and you refused the order of your commanding general! You are a war correspondent and I am

Commander-in-Chief. I give orders and you follow them! Yesterday we had a flag-raising ceremony and no photographer! And two French destroyers came by and saluted, and no photographer!"

I tried to explain to the general that as an American correspondent I was free to choose the unit I would cover, that I had been with General Monsabert's division during the battle for Siena, and that I wanted to go with his men when they landed in France. But my reasoning simply inflamed him and he began to shout that if I refused to obey his command to come with him, if I remained on General Monsabert's ship, he would give orders that I not be allowed to take a single picture in France. I would be forbidden to ride in any vehicle. "I shall see that you cannot work in France!" he shouted.

I was dismissed to await the general's pleasure. But tactful diplomacy on the part of his aides eventually soothed him and he became a different man. When I was summoned to his quarters again I found him smiling and apologetic. There had been a misunderstanding. The day before, Martha Gellhorn Hemingway, who was reporting for *Collier's,* had visited his ship and told him there was "a great American photographer" on another ship. And he had decided I would come with him. "I wanted my own special pet war correspondent," he said, "and you would be it."

Then he gave me his blessings and wished me good luck in the landing. "When you are in France, come to see me." And he kissed me on both cheeks.

This sort of wartime contact, whether earned in combat or through caprice, has meant a great deal to me over the years. When I left the European theater to fly to the Philippines in November, 1944, it was to rejoin General Douglas MacArthur, who had just landed in Leyte. I had last been with the general in Manila during the first Japanese attacks of the war three years earlier. I covered his Leyte campaign and was the only still photographer to accompany him on the U.S.S. *Boise,* his command ship, for the invasion of Luzon. And I was invited to go ashore with him.

As our landing craft neared the beach I saw that the SeaBees had gotten there before us and had laid a pontoon walkway out from the beach. As we headed for it, I climbed the boat's ramp and jumped onto the pontoons so that I could photograph MacArthur as he walked ashore. But in the instant of my jumping I heard the boat's engines reversing and, swinging around, I saw the boat rapidly backing away. Judging what was happening, I raced to the beach and ran dry-shod some hundred yards along it and stood waiting for the boat to come to me. When it did it dropped its ramp in knee-deep water and I photographed MacArthur wading ashore. No one I have ever known in public life had a better understanding of the drama and power of a picture.

Soon after that landing at Lingayen Gulf on Luzon we started our push south for Manila, where the most important story of my entire coverage lay ahead of me. The first objective MacArthur had set for the advance units entering the city was the liberation of the civilian prison camp, Santo Tomas. It was my own prison camp. I had been a prisoner there for the first eight months of the war, before my transfer to a camp in China and eventual repatriation home.

The 37th Division and the First Cavalry were moving south abreast of each other, each determined to be the first into Manila. There was intense rivalry between them and when word got out that MacArthur had given the 37th the mission of racing ahead to take the city, nearly all of the war correspondents flocked to it, finding places in the long, drawn-out mechanized columns. And I was among them.

But then, on the first night out, Colonel Herb Wheeler, who was on MacArthur's staff and an old combat friend, found me in the early tropical dusk and, pulling me aside, said in a low voice, "Keep this under your hat, but the Old Man's just given the First Cav the order to be first in Manila."

I switched to the First Cav and found myself with only four other correspondents on this climactic story, and I the only photojournalist. We knifed through the Japanese lines and the Japanese blew a bridge behind us. And from then on we had the story to ourselves. When we reached my old prison camp I climbed onto the lead tank to show the way through the compound. And when we entered the main building I was back again among old friends. The picture of the two starved men ravaged by beriberi shows two of my old roommates as they looked the day we liberated them (p. 118).

Soon after Manila was taken, atom bombs were dropped on Hiroshima and Nagasaki, and the Japanese, already pounded by massive raids throughout the home islands, offered to surrender. Because of long-standing friendships I was able to land in Japan with the first American contingent and to be in the lead jeep as we encountered our defeated enemy (pp. 122, 123).

I stayed on to cover the American occupation at a time when many of General MacArthur's wartime staff were still with him in GHQ. They tended to grant correspondents access to good stories—and to the general—on the basis of how long the correspondents had been with his command. Since my coverage began in the Philippines in 1941, before the Japanese attack, I was included among the most privileged: "the old Bataan crowd."

Much of this attitude came down from the general himself, who was more conscious of the press and their coverage than any other military man I have known. His decisions were often arbitrary and he didn't care a bit about complaints of favoritism. When he decided to jump an outfit of the 11th Airborne Division over Pyongyang in Korea in 1950, he called in five correspondents and invited us to go along with him (p. 190). All of us had been with his command some years and he had no compunction about the exclusive he was giving us. His aides answered all complaints from our competition with "That's the general's decision, and that's the way it is."

When a new Pentagon regulation stipulated that correspondents accredited to Occupation headquarters were limited to thirty days' absence from that theater on pain of losing their accreditation, I faced a problem. I often left Japan to cover the civil war in China, and at this moment I was leaving for the Philippines and Indonesia. So I went to see the general and told him that I might be away for more than thirty days. What would the consequences be?

"You've got no problem about the Philippines," he told me. "That's our area. As for Indonesia, don't worry about it. If you overstay, I'll cover up for you."

In this book—a picture odyssey of prints chosen from three decades of photoreporting around the world —there is a gap of nearly two years: 1942 and 1943. I was thirty-four years old then and had come a long way toward my goal as a journalist and recorder of the behavior of our time. And when the war with Japan began, in December, 1941, I was exactly where I should have been: in Manila under Japanese attack.

For nearly a year before that, with my wife Shelley, who was the other half of our writer-photographer team, we had been covering China and the Sino-Japanese war. Then, as the signals increased that Japanese attacks on Southeast Asia might be imminent, we left Chungking late in 1941 and went to Burma, Singapore, Malaya, and then, fatefully, on to the Philippines.

There we found General MacArthur trying to build an army out of promises and a willing people who were lacking in materiel and training. The sense of approaching war was very strong and we were not reassured when an officer on MacArthur's staff told us that we should be ready to hold off an attack "by March." That was three months away, and we got the impression that he thought the Japanese would wait that long. But of course they didn't.

In a state of tense activity we shipped our story on the preparations for war in the Philippines. It went on what was to be the last commercial plane to fly out of Manila in four years. And just before the cables were blown and all communications cut we received a message from New York that the story had arrived and was the lead in *LIFE* for that week. But by then the Japanese had drawn a net around Manila and we were trapped.

Then suddenly I was sitting on a concrete floor in a prison camp without a camera in my hands, a dream gone out of me. Everything had stopped for me while outside the world was still going on. It was the most difficult period of my life, especially the first weeks, when the war raged nearby on Bataan and Corregidor and Japanese planes flew overhead and the sounds of bombing and artillery fire came into the camp night and day.

I lost two years of covering the world. But I have made peace with the experience. And I know that if the Japanese had not taken me out of the war I might not have had the following years to watch and photograph all the people and places and events that continue to be my life.

Carl Mydans aboard landing craft with General MacArthur en route from command ship U.S.S. Boise *to assault beaches at Lingayen in the Philippines on D-day, January 9, 1945.*

TALKING TO CARL MYDANS

BY PHILIP B. KUNHARDT, JR., SUMMER 1984

"If I wanted a series of wars covered and had to pick just one photographer out of the hundreds I've known to do it, I'd pick Carl."

That's the opinion of Edward K. Thompson. Ed is the dean of magazine journalism, having run *LIFE* from the late '40s to the early '60s before creating *Smithsonian* magazine and editing it for over a decade. So Ed knows what he's talking about. He's talking here about Carl Mydans, photographer.

"I don't think he is a natural photographer," Thompson continues. "But he's always used his intelligence to make himself a good photographer. He's learned everything. He's always experimenting. He's terribly resourceful. He's managed to be in most of the right places at most of the right times. If I were playing it for reliability, I'd put him at the top. But it's unfair to categorize him as just a war photographer. He's *all-around*."

So that's the man I'm talking to here—Carl Mydans, 77 years old now, a man who has photographed almost every kind of event in his lifetime, but especially war. A professional his editors could always count on. Smart. Courageous. The Best.

In between working on the layouts for this book and making the selections for the Mydans retrospective exhibition, Carl and I talked together on three separate mornings. He discussed his life. I listened and asked some questions that I thought needed asking. What follows is my version of what was said. Interspersed is a listing of pertinent biographical milestones in Carl Mydans' life.

Born Boston, May 20, 1907. Grandfather a bookbinder in village near Odessa who came to America to escape cruelty of Tsar. Father a professional musician. Family moved to Medford, Massachusetts, on Mystic River, where Carl worked in boatyards after school and on weekends. Sold local stories to *Medford Daily Mercury* for three dollars apiece. Later sold stories to *Boston Globe* and *Boston Herald* before graduating from Boston University School of Journalism at 23. Worked as a reporter in New York

Carl and Shelley Mydans with British Indian troops of the Hyderabad Regiment in Singapore in April 1941. Virtually all these troops died in battle when the Japanese overran Malaya and Singapore some eight months later. By this time the Mydanses had left for the Philippines, where they were captured and imprisoned by the Japanese in January 1942.

City. Took course in photography at Brooklyn Institute of Arts and Sciences. Bought secondhand Zeiss Contax with 50mm/1.5 lens. July 12, 1935: recruited by government to work for Department of Interior's Resettlement Administration, which merged into Farm Security Administration. Photographed rural poor for FSA all over country. November 15, 1936: hired by *LIFE* magazine while first issue was going to press. *LIFE* had seen a good thing: this short, strong, thin, swarthy, exuberant, determined young man had an open mind, a feel for history, a knowledge of his camera and what he could do with it, a willingness to go anywhere for a story.

Q. You have written, Carl, that as a boy you were fascinated by what hands could do and make. You wanted to be a shipbuilder once and then you wanted to be a surgeon. Your father was a musician and you were intrigued by the play of his hands upon his oboe. Instead of a saw or a scalpel or a musical instrument, the object that finally satisfied your desire to do something productive and creative and maybe even beautiful with your hands was your camera. Can you talk about your camera and your feelings for it?

A. I began using a camera seriously, one might say professionally, when I was at Boston University and I was hired by their publicity department and the job that the few of us had there was known as "hometowning." We would write stories about B.U. students and we'd send them to their hometown newspapers. It turned out that they also needed some pictures, so they asked me if I'd ever used a camera and I said a Brownie. They brought out a Graflex, a huge box with a mirror, and I learned how to use it and made pictures for Boston University now and again. My next use of a camera was in New York when I was working for the newspaper *American Banker*. During my off hours I worked with my newly bought secondhand camera— a Contax. In those days there were two 35mm cameras. One was the Leica and the other was the Contax.

When I began to use my 35mm camera, I was never separated from it. I wore it often under my jacket, on my shoulder like a weapon in a holster. I always had the feeling from the time I got up in the morning until I went back to bed at night that something was going to happen in front of me, and when it did, I wanted my camera to be there.

When I came to know Tom McAvoy, who was with the *Washington Herald* then and later was chosen to be one of the original photographers for *LIFE*, I found he was never separated from his Leica also, even though he was disdained by news photographers because he had what was known within the photographic circle as "that goddamned little toy."

Years later, when I lived in China, the very feel of that camera made me compare it to the Chinese I saw feeling and holding pieces of jade. I couldn't understand why that jade meant so much to them. They would carry it in their pockets and they would keep it up their sleeves and every little while they would take the jade out and hold it in their hands. It was sensuous. In a way, when I felt my own camera, I was like the Chinese handling a piece of jade.

Q. You also used it during certain difficult or dangerous stories, I'm sure, to distance yourself from your subjects.

A. That's true. And I think it is fair to say that all war photographers hide behind their cameras. I hid behind mine for years and years and years. It was a shield. I held it in front of me. All war photographers have done that any number of times in combat when they found themselves in bad situations. War photographers put themselves into these situations. They are not like a soldier or an officer and someone says we want you to get into that line. You arbitrarily say well, gee, I think there is a good story there. And then you get in there and things go all right, but every now and again you don't think you are going to get out and you think this is very serious and you say to yourself what am I doing here. It's at those moments especially when your camera stands as your protection, stands there in front of you, between you and danger. I think that the photographer in combat has a greater protection than the soldier who has a rifle in his hand. That camera has unbelievable protective power.

Q. You have said, Carl, that a man named Bob Cheney whom you worked for in his boatyard as a teenager, and Roy Stryker whom you worked for at the Farm Security Administration, were the most important influences in your life. They both taught you the importance of excellence and how to see things when you look at them. What does that mean—how to see things?

A. I think involved in that is not only looking at something but looking for perfection. Perfection is a high goal for photographers. Bob Cheney was a boatbuilder who taught me how to use my hands, and he would often stop me and say, stand back and look at it, and if you think you've done a good job, that's it. If you don't think you've done a good job, then go back and redo it or do it better next time.

Those are words that I have never forgotten, and whenever I have looked at a picture or looked at the possibility of a picture that I am going to make I often hear his words. Will what I take meet my expectations? He didn't say meet *his* expectations, he said meet *my* expectations. It was one of the most profound things that ever was said to me.

Roy Stryker had a very similar characteristic about *is this good or is this bad?* He would sometimes pick up a picture that I made and look at it. He was an intense, visual historian. And he would say I like that picture but that lamppost there in the foreground, I don't like that. Don't tell me that it was there. I don't want to know anything about a picture that isn't right. I want you to make a picture that *is right*.

Q. Carl, how did you get involved with Time Inc.?

A. It was with a picture I made on Wall Street in my lunch hour. A young man named Eugene Daniell was standing on a soapbox, one of the earliest of agitators against this country, a Harvard graduate who was saying things were not equal. He was talking to a small crowd. I asked someone who is he. And somebody said he's the guy who last year threw a stink bomb into the ventilating system of the Stock Exchange, stopped the Stock Exchange for the first time in business hours since World War I.

I took his picture and went back to my little room in Brooklyn Heights and developed it there, at night. Then I washed my prints in a common bathroom that three other roomers and I shared on the fourth floor of 170 Columbia Heights. Often they would come and say, Carl, I want to take a shower, can you take the prints out of the bathtub?

First I went to the AP [Associated Press] and then the UP [United Press] to sell the picture of Eugene Daniell. Nobody wanted it. So I finally decided well, gee, maybe I will go to one of those newsweekly magazines. And I went to *Time.*

I was expecting to be turned away, but I was met by the woman who was the receptionist—whom I came to know years and years after that—Sally Harrington, who was so nice to me. She said I've got just the person to send you to. And she sent me up to *Time*'s floor, where I was met by a woman and my heart fell. Women are not the people for anybody to show pictures to, I thought. She turned out to be Mary Fraser, later to be Mary Longwell, who was such an important force at *LIFE* magazine. She said to me oh I know who will be interested in you. And she sent me to the editor Dan Longwell.

Longwell was wonderful to me. He looked at the picture, asked me questions about it. He said gee, we're interested in this and he said to me what kind of camera did you take it with. I said I took it with a Contax, and he said, ah, a 35mm camera, I want to tell you that's the new wave here. He said I am going to keep this picture, and he used it the next week. It was the first picture I had published. And then I got assignments from Dan Longwell. One of the first assignments after that was to go to Ossining, New York, and photograph a man who had just built a better snake and rat trap. And *Time* magazine used that picture, too.

Q. Tell me a bit about your FSA days.

A. I may have been the only Farm Security Administration photographer traveling around the United States making pictures who refused to go to bed each night until he developed his shooting for that day. I would pick the little hotels, overnight rest camps, wherever I saw a sign saying "ice-cold running water." I needed that ice-cold running water for developing. I carried with me in my car a developing kit and chemicals. The more I developed the browner my fingernails got, and I learned to be very careful not to get the developer on my shirt or my trousers because the next morning they would have a brown stain.

Q. In all those months of traveling and taking pictures in the West and the Midwest and the New England states and in the South, you must have gotten quite a great feeling for the country and for the people.

A. Yes, it is true, and especially for the faces of the people, because of one of the things that Roy Stryker said to me before sending me out. You will see that this is a period of disaster in the United States, he said, and I want you to take pictures of everything you can find of what's happened to the people. I think you are going to find what is happening in the faces of the people. . . .I did, and what I mostly photographed in those months of travel in America was people and their faces.

Q. Then just as Time Inc.'s secret new picture magazine—"Project X" they called it—was starting up under the name that was finally chosen for it—*LIFE*—you were hired. You were the fifth *LIFE* photographer.

A. Yes, and immediately Dan Longwell sent me to Hollywood to cover movies.

Twenty-nine-year-old Mydans arrived in Hollywood by train November 22, 1936. He photographed the making of the Paramount movie *Souls at Sea* starring Gary Cooper and George Raft and Frances Dee. First and last soft assignment. February, 1937, to Texas for numerous stories, including last great cattle drive and tough oil towns. Without a home of his own, Mydans lived out of hotel rooms as his assignments in 1937 and 1938 took him to Georgia, Pennsylvania, Florida, West Virginia, New York, New

Jersey, Vermont, Washington, California, Texas, Maryland, Illinois, and the Caribbean. On June 19, 1938, he married a bright and pretty *LIFE* researcher, Shelley Smith, from California. Carl got the tough stories, those requiring stamina, know-how, and strength. War rumbled in Europe. Shelley and Carl were made a reporter-photographer team by *LIFE* and on September 13, 1939, left for Europe on Pan American's Flying Clipper to cover fighting wherever it might occur. Russian invasion of Finland was first. Then to Fascist Italy, to a falling France, and, on July 4, 1940, back to the States. To China in early 1941. Covered Sino-Japanese war out of bomb-pummeled Chungking. Covered stories all over Southeast Asia. Captured by Japanese in January, 1942, and imprisoned in Manila. After eight and a half months moved in Japanese troop ship to Shanghai. Interned again by Japanese. 1943: freed and sent home. 1944: the Italian and French campaigns. November: return to Pacific. Leyte Campaign. 1945: Leyte, Luzon, Okinawa. Finally the Japanese surrender.

Q. What were the circumstances, Carl, under which you started being a war photographer?

A. When the war in Europe was on the horizon, I was working at Wright Field in Dayton, Ohio, doing a story for *LIFE* magazine on some of the most advanced aircraft we were building, under the restrictions of security.

As I went out there each day working in the various hangars, I could hear the radios talking about what was happening all over the world. I was there in one of those hangars the day it was announced that the Germans had invaded Poland, which turned out to be the beginning of World War II.

I had a phone call from Wilson Hicks, I think it was, to finish the story I was doing as quickly as I could. We want to talk with you in New York, he said. I came in and then there was a talk first with Dan Longwell and then with Hicks. At virtually the same time Mary Fraser talked with Shelley. They were thinking about sending us overseas together as a team.

Finally, as the war spread, they decided they would send us overseas, but as always, as you know, at *LIFE* magazine no decision is ever made until there isn't time to go home and get your toothbrush. Then someone thought about sending us over with gas masks, and in some way this new and promising magazine was able to inveigle from the army two gas masks, one for Shelley and one for me. Mary Fraser gave Shelley a gift of a money belt and Wilson Hicks gave me a money belt, but nobody remembered we needed visas.

Somehow we made it to Europe, though, and then because the French and the Germans sat quietly watching each other in what became known as the "phony war," we were sent to London. It was while we were working there on Britain preparing for war that the news suddenly came that the Russians had bombed Helsinki, and that was really the beginning of my wartime career.

Nobody knew what it was all about, so I left almost at once and went to Stockholm. While I was there I bought some winter gear. I took a train from Stockholm as far north as the train would go to a town that was across the Tornea River from a Finnish town called Tornea. It was wintertime and I soon learned that all one did to get to Finland was to go out on the ice and walk across the river, which I did.

The first battlefield I ever saw was at the Kemi River. I came in when the battle was almost over, but there was shooting all around and bodies everywhere, frozen, some wounded, where an entire Russian division had been surrounded and destroyed in that forest. The Russian division, newly activated in Leningrad, was inexperienced. It was led by one tank and the soldiers were in deep snow and the wagons were pulled by horses going down one narrow road in the forest, north of the Arctic Circle in minus-twenty-degree temperature. It was in the winter darkness, so there was only a short period of light in every twenty-four hours. The sun would get just above the horizon and then disappear again. The Finns were superior fighters and they were dressed in white snowsuits so they couldn't be seen. They simply crawled up on their bellies and blew the tracks off the lead tank, and crawled up on their bellies and blew the tracks off the rear tank, and the whole division was caught in the forest and slowly destroyed. My pictures showed the dead bodies, the frozen bodies of the Russians and their horses.

And what happened was the whole world was misinformed, misled by this great Finnish victory over the Russians because nobody knew what the circumstances were, and they began to sit back in comfort thinking the Finns could handle the Russians. Of course the Finns were the size of a plum and the Russians were the size of orchards.

I covered the war from the beginning to the end. Thirty days is all that war took. I shipped my film out to Sweden in takes. Shelley came to Stockholm and received it and edited it and captioned it and sent it to New York.

Q. Did you have many problems up there, taking pictures and developing the negatives?

A. I developed every day. I brought along the same little developing kit I used when I was working for the Farm Security Administration and, just as I had developed my own film at the end of each day or in the middle of the night back then, whenever I got back to the tiny little hotel room I had at Rovaniemi I developed my film and was able myself to judge and see what I was doing—in lighting conditions I had never worked in before. There was almost no sun, and when it did come for a very short while it was a feeble tinkle of light just showing above the horizon.

No manual had been written about taking pictures in conditions like that. I had to learn everything by trial and error. My shutter would freeze and in the beginning I often couldn't use my cameras when I wanted desperately to take pictures. I wore a heavy Swedish sheepskin coat and I learned to keep both cameras inside it, and if I took them out for a picture one at a time and got them back inside fast, I could usually operate. In most cases I had to size up the picture I wanted, sight it out, reach into my coat and take out one of my cameras quickly, focus quickly, and put it back under my coat. Sometimes the shutter wouldn't work at all because of the cold, and I had to learn also to judge the speed of my shutter by its sound, because the shutter no longer worked according to what the setting was on the camera.

I had to show everything I took to the censors to get the stuff out. One of the evils of that censorship was that you could show as many dead Russians as you wanted but you could not show a dead Finn, or hardly even a wounded Finn. So the impression was gained in the outside world not to worry about the Finns because they were handling the Russians very well. Look at all these dead Russians—the Finns are great. They can handle them.

That was my first experience in war and since it was the first time I ever saw dead on the field, it left permanent effects. I still think of it. Since then I have seen many dead, many battlefields, but that first experience left the deepest scars.

Q. Tell me, Carl, about covering war in China.

A. We were on our own there. We were based in the interior at Chungking. Nearly all the foreign journalists lived in what was called the press hostel: fifteen to eighteen of us from various countries who lived in little adobe mud huts with straw roofs—no running water or sewerage. The heart of the story was in Chungking, which in the first months we were there was bombed by the Japanese virtually every day and often at night. The Chinese had no anti-aircraft that could reach the Japanese planes. When the air-raid warnings came, everybody simply fled into deep tunnels that were built into the rocky areas of Chungking. I had all my equipment with me and many months of supplies of film because we were cut off by the Japanese. When the bombers came, we would run down into the shelters. I had hired Chinese boys who would take my camera equipment and supplies out of our room and carry them down into one of the shelters so that if the compound was struck and burned we wouldn't lose our equipment. Once our little mud hut was hit directly and nearly everything that was still in it was destroyed, but fortunately my gear was saved.

When we went on journalistic trips outside Chungking, traveling on what they call public buses, which were simply old open trucks with tops fashioned to them, we carried with us all our equipment and the most minimal living supplies. The inflation in Chungking was so great that the value of the Chinese dollar changed hourly. When we were going away, let's say on a two- or three-week trip, and had to take all the money that we would need with us, we changed our U.S. dollars in the bank at Chungking, and each of us carried a small knapsack on our back that had nothing in it but Chinese currency.

Another thing we carried were tung-oil sheets. Tung oil comes from the tung tree and is used to paint Chinese furniture. Interestingly, many people are allergic to it. We carried tung-oil sheets because there is a legend that the oil repels bedbugs, and bedbugs were anathema to anybody who stayed at inns on the byways of China. Everywhere that there were people there were bedbugs. At night when we lay down in a little inn room, we would place the tung-oil sheets under us to keep the bedbugs from attacking. Bedbugs are a common institutional creature and they are especially a prison camp bug. When we were in prison camps, first in the Philippines and then in China, we coped as everybody else coped with bedbugs. They were in all our beds, on our clothes, and it was not uncommon to be sitting down somewhere talking with someone, to see a bedbug crawling out of his collar over his neck. I am an old hand at bedbugs.

In China we always traveled light because of the photographic equipment. That always came first. Other needs that competed in weight or bulk had to be left behind. Shelley, poor soul, suffered all those years traveling with me and with my equipment. Often we left books, shoes, clothing behind, but never cameras and never film.

Q. I want you to give me a picture of yourself as a war photographer, if you can, Carl. Pretend that you are another reporter back in the days when you were a war correspondent and you are looking at Carl Mydans: you have to write a story on him, you have to describe him, how he lives in the field, how he works, how he thinks, you have to describe his techniques.

A. All right, I'll try to get into it. I'll stand back and look at him. I've known him a long time.

Well, I think I've already told you about my interest in the historical importance of what I'm reporting and my identification with the people I photograph. So I try to bring to my coverage a certain amount of background as well as the immediate visual or emotional impact. But as far as the technique of my work in the field goes, how I actually operated in combat, of course my cameras and film came first. I slept with them beside me and when it rained I huddled with them under my poncho. I held them above the rising water in a foxhole as one would hold a child, and when I fell or threw myself on the ground for cover I always took the blow, not the cameras.

As well as my photographic gear I carried a lightweight poncho, and I wore a canteen and canteen cup with a spoon tucked in it and a first-aid kit attached to my pistol belt. In my pocket I carried a jackknife with a can opener and screwdriver that had never been separated from me since I was a small boy until the Japanese took it away from me when I was captured in the Philippines. Those things and my helmet were all I needed to live in the field. The helmet came with an inner liner and an outer steel cover, and I used that cover as a bucket to bathe from and do my laundry in as well as to protect me from shells and bullets. Now, as we so often try to make good things "better," we have developed a helmet that is all one piece—I don't know how the soldiers in the field handle this development.

My camera bag was a musette bag, and for years and years I used the same musette bag that I got at Abercrombie & Fitch. It was a large bag that took all my cameras and most of my film, though I always kept some extra film stashed away someplace in case anything happened to the film in the bag. Also folded up in the back of it were some special bright-red shipping envelopes and some sealing tape, because I might get someplace where I had to send my story back to headquarters, to be shipped by someone who might not have a shipping envelope, especially one prepared with the directions , "For LIFE magazine from Carl Mydans," and the warning, "Photographic Film. Do not X-ray. Rush."

Sometimes I was lucky enough to run into some other correspondent who was on his way back to headquarters, or wherever the shipping area was, who would take my story in for me. And when I was going back myself I would always turn around and say, I'm going in, anybody got any film, anybody got any copy to go.

When you are a war photographer for a publication, there are three important things: the first is to get where the action is and to photograph it. The second is to get that film back from where you've been shooting and on the way to your home office. No story, no matter how well you have done it, is worth anything unless you can get it back to transportation, and to your publication.

A third is to keep a careful record of what you have photographed. I always carried a notebook with me. I had trained myself to use one from the earliest years working with the Farm Security Administration. I made notes on everything, every roll of film I shot and, if I could, every frame on each roll, with enough background so that I could transcribe those notes into running captions of what the shipment contained, what outfit I was with, what the action was, the roll number and the frame number. Because I was almost always working with two cameras, there would be two rolls of film that would have similar messages, similar captions on them, but they might be different because one camera would have a longer lens than the other or include different subjects, so I would sometimes couple my captions, saying that roll six and seven go together and you will find on them such and such pictures. Many times the captions were just as important as the film. Many of us making very good pictures of action in very difficult circumstances were unable to get sufficient captions down between taking our film out of our camera and giving it to someone to take in for shipment. Then, even though the film got to New York, if someone could not make head or tail out of what you had, it was not usable, and so there was worship of captions in the field. Then there was another thing that was necessary—a message when the film went off. You would send a brief cable to your office saying, "from Mydans, shipment 16, leaving Southern Italy today with coverage of the Third Division in its attack on Velletri." Some of these words would be cut by censors, but there would be enough in there for the editors in New York to know what you were doing, and in return for that cable you would then get a cable from New York saying your shipment 16 received today. When you got that back you were comforted by two things —you knew that they had gotten the shipment and, just as important, you saw nothing in the message that said you were having equipment trouble. Remember, equipment trouble is a constant problem for anybody working in the field, especially working in the field under difficult situations—in the rain, crossing rivers, your cameras being banged around, your falling on your cameras, that kind of thing—and especially when you are using a 35mm camera where all the mechanisms are as refined as those in fine watches. There is no way to know that if you drop your camera or you fall on it whether everything is still in good working order. So you scrutinize the messages that come back to you. If they just say, "Your shipment has been received," it goes without saying that everything is okay. But it might say, "Look back in your notes on roll number six. We think camera number two has shutter trouble." Then you'd know there was something wrong and your pictures weren't turning out. There are a lot of unknowns in this, but if you have followed what you are doing carefully, you probably can trace what's wrong.

As you can see, I am meticulous in what I do. I do my homework. If there is time when I am sent somewhere to do a story, I go to the library and look up what I can find. In the days before the Xerox was invented, I would sit down and scribble out things as fast as I could. Today, thank God for the Xerox. Now I go and find as many clippings as I can and Xerox them and read them on the plane or in the car. I become an historian in events that have taken place surrounding the assignment and I try very hard to relate what *has* happened to what *is* happening.

When I was covering the war in Italy in 1944, I had all kinds of little notes, all kinds of clippings, and an Italian travel guidebook with me so that when I got into a town I could sit down and read the history of the town—see what various conquerors had been there before—so that when I looked at things I saw a second dimension. I think that is the way I should put it—there was always a second dimension to what I was looking at. If I had the time and the opportunity to mention what had happened there before and how that was related to what was happening now, I would try to do that. When we entered Rome with Mark Clark's Fifth Army, the first two or three days in Rome I just forgot about what was happening and went off and did the G.I.s only as they related to great monumental arenas of Italy. I tried to relate that period of the war in some way to what Rome had been.

Q. Carl, you were always pretty free to do what you wanted to do when you were covering a war, weren't you? I mean, you could cover this action or that action or you could decide not to. Weren't some of the choices very difficult? Could you talk about choices?

A. You must remember the way the United States Army worked in those days. There was always a Public

Relations headquarters with units of the Army. Each division, regiment, brigade had their own PRO—now called PIO. That headquarters provided the logistics for any of the correspondents who were attached to its units. There was always a place to go if the correspondents were not actually out with the fighting units. There was always a PRO mess tent and a PRO billet tent or a house they had taken over where you could get a bunk and a shower, where you could eat, where you could ship your film or copy from. And there, correspondents would be briefed any number of times a day depending upon whether there was action or developments. There were some correspondents, especially wire service correspondents, who never left the unit's headquarters. Their job was not to go out into the field and see action but to get the word from the headquarters public relations officers, who would declare three or four times a day that their front had advanced three miles or that there was a fight going on at such and such a place. And since we were accredited to the units we were with and whatever we did—text or pictures—went through their censorship, there were no military developments that were kept from us. We were part of the unit and they were not concerned that we were going to break any military secrets. So we would hear from them every day what was happening. If we were back at PRO headquarters for the night, when we got up in the morning, got shaved, got our breakfast—often long before that, as we rolled out of our bunks—we would hear that there was a big fight going on at such and such a place. There was always a division headquarters map or a public relations map where we could see what was happening and who was in command. We learned whether we were under attack or whether we were attacking, learned who was being hurt, learned whether it was a good or a bad place to go, and each correspondent, each war photographer, had to make his own decision whether or not that was the place for him.

One little incident comes back to me that will show you what we were up against. I was in Italy, and I was with a small group of war correspondents and war photographers. Included by chance in the small group I was with were Eric Sevareid of CBS and Ed Morgan of ABC. We had been with a division that was in great trouble and we were under attack a good part of the day. It was beginning to come to the end of the day, always the worst part of the day for me in the field, because it means thinking about where are you going to be that night and what is going to happen to you that night. We went to get a briefing from the divisional commander outside his tent; he had set up a map board and told us what was happening, and he said we are going to be hurt tonight, and we think—and I am going to tell you quite frankly—we're going to be badly hurt. You fellows have got to make up your minds whether you want to stay here with us or go back six or eight kilometers and come here in the morning. We think if you leave here tonight, now, before it gets too dark, you can find out in the morning whether we're still here or not. My suggestion to you, of course, is that you clear out of here tonight. It is going to be dark in about an hour and you are not going to see anything that is going to happen. We stand a good chance of being overrun, and in the morning you will be in much better shape to come in here and see what happened to us and report on it. We thanked him and we got into a circle and began to talk over whether we were going to stay there or not. As far as the photographers were concerned, we weren't going to lose anything, because we couldn't make pictures at night. So it was agreed, what the hell, let's get out of here, and we went back six to eight kilometers. When we came back in the morning they were all there and they hadn't been hurt at all, but the circumstances of the battle had changed. This will give you an illustration of how touchy the whole thing was. Each correspondent had to decide for himself, is it worth it for me to stay here through this battle, I may see a great deal of important stuff or I may not see much and the chances are that we are going to be overrun and destroyed, so is it wiser to go back six kilometers and come in and join them again. This is the kind of decision we were making all the time.

I remember when we were on Leyte with MacArthur and we got briefed one day by General Diller about a top secret landing on Luzon that was coming up. It was the beginning of the end of the war in the Pacific. And General Diller told us that it was going to be a rough landing but here you are, gentlemen, take your pick, you can go in with any one of four or five first-wave assaults—you can go in with PT boats, you can go in with destroyers, you can go in with a parachute drop behind the lines. Bill Chickering of *Time* magazine and I were going to go on an amphibious first-wave landing together. But then I picked MacArthur's name out of the hat to be the still man to go with him on the landing and only five of us of the correspondent corps could go with him. When Bill Chickering learned that I had gotten MacArthur, which was a big thing as far as picture coverage was concerned, and I was in a privileged spot for getting him going ashore, Bill changed his mind. He came up to me as we were parting there on the waterfront and said, "I decided not to go in on an amphibious landing. Since you're not going in with me, I think I've got a good spot on the *New Mexico*. And so I am going to go in and do the coverage from the *New Mexico*."

Now that's the choice that any of us could have made and I might have made the same choice he did, I don't know. All I know is that Bill chose not to go in the amphibious landing. Instead he chose the *New Mexico*, and he was killed on the bridge by kamikazes. That just shows you how touch-and-go these decisions are. Some guys have a sixth sense in knowing what to do and get away with it, while for others the number is up. One never knows.

The major difference between a war photographer going into combat and a member of the Armed Forces is that the soldier or the marine has no choice. I have sometimes thought in my years in combat how much I appreciated the fact that I could do whatever I wanted to do, but often I wished I didn't have the choice. For instance, I didn't want to go back those six or eight kilometers that night in Italy—that is still in my mind. And if I had had no choice, I wouldn't have had the uneasiness of going back.

Of course, there's the soldier's side of it, too. I remember when we made the landing at Lingayen we went in standing up, but that night when we had gotten a lot of our equipment ashore, the Japanese who had zeroed in on the beach began to shell us, and there was no way out of it, except to spend the night there and take it. I hadn't dug a foxhole or anything, so finally I jumped into somebody else's foxhole and damn near killed a couple of guys who were in there. They grunted and groaned and complained and finally, after lying there a while, knowing that we couldn't get out of it because we were being heavily shelled, one of them said who in the hell are you. I said I'm a war correspondent and he said, gee, a war correspondent, what do you do here and I said I take pictures, and he said, you mean to say that you're a civilian and you're in here and I said yes, and he said do you have to be in here, and I said . . . no, a war correspondent can go anywhere he wants. He said Jesus . . . would I love your job, and I said why would you love my job, here we both are in the same foxhole, both scared stiff and both wishing we weren't here and he said, yeah, I know all that, but if I were a war correspondent, I'd get up and get the hell out of here.

Q. Carl, you were considered to be a "pal" of General MacArthur. When he first fulfilled his famous "I shall return" by wading ashore in the Philippines, you weren't around, so three months later he waded ashore again on another landing and you were able to make what is probably your most famous picture. Can you tell me something about MacArthur and your special relationship to him?

A. I thought he was the most brilliant military man I had ever known. And one of the most brilliant just plain men, too, because of the way his mind worked. I had good moments with him and bad moments. I was covering the campaign in Italy until I got a coded message from *LIFE* magazine saying something like we think it is time you would like to go back to the Pacific and I read into that very carefully worded statement that MacArthur was going to land in the Philippines. I flew back and soon I was covering him. He was a stickler for his own rules. Take pictures of me while I'm working, he told me. I will not allow you into my headquarters or home. I don't believe in posed pictures, he said. MacArthur believed in giving complete, faithful support to any of his friends. He could not conceive that a correspondent whom he liked would ever say or do anything about him that was not fully supportive. So when I was the Tokyo Time-Life bureau chief in 1947 and did a story on the Supreme Commander that included something critical about how he was handling labor in Japan, I soon heard he didn't like the story. His right-hand man General Courtney Whitney called me up and said Carl, I'd like you to come up here, we want to talk to you, and I came up. I never saw MacArthur that day; Whitney was going to give me the message. He held up a copy of the latest edition of *Time* and, slapping it with his hand, he said to me Carl, this is the first time we knew that we were nursing a viper to our bosom. And I said but why Court? And he said this story is so critical and unfair to the Old Man. We never thought you would write a story like this. Shortly after that Shelley and I were among the correspondents invited to come to lunch at the American Embassy. As the correspondents came through the main doors of the big dining room, Douglas MacArthur stood with Mrs. MacArthur beside him. When we came up, Mrs. MacArthur said and here are Carl and Shelley. And the general looked at us and said how do you do, Mr. and Mrs. Mydans. He hadn't called us by anything but by our first names for years. That was his way of telling us what he thought of our story.

Another indication of the kind of person MacArthur was is this story, and you won't hear it from many people. It was 1947 or going into 1948 now and I was leaving Tokyo to do a big story on the revival of Japanese industry. I put all my cameras into the back of my car and went up into the office to check if there were any last-minute cables. When I got down again, the car had been stolen, with all my cameras in it. I reported it to the provost marshal's office and ran back to the office and as I was entering, I heard my secretary on the telephone saying, just a minute, General Whitney, he's just come through the door. I picked up the telephone and General Whitney said Carl, the Old Man has just had word that your car was stolen and with it all your cameras, and he just said to me *get Carl's cameras back*. And I said gee, Court, how did the general learn so quickly. He said never mind about that, just get me a list of your cameras and I will get it out to the police in every prefecture of Japan. In the end I got back every single camera, which is a mark of what MacArthur not only did for people whom he liked but how he was so quickly aware of everything that happened to them.

I'll tell you another instance of how he seemed to know everything immediately. In 1950 I was coming to the end of my period in Asia and had come home to talk to Ed Thompson and to get ready to make the switch from Asia to the U.S. I was to be on a radio program in New York talking about Korea, and just before going on the air a reporter came to me and said gee, Carl, you're sure coming on this program at just the right time, the North Koreans have just invaded South Korea. I picked up the phone and called Ed Thompson and asked how soon he wanted me to go back, and he said as soon as I was finished with the radio program.

David Douglas Duncan was in Japan at the time doing a story and he flew to Korea while I was on my way back after the radio program, and MacArthur flew in from Tokyo. When MacArthur got out of his plane, Duncan went up to him and introduced himself and said I am with *LIFE* magazine, I am Carl's replacement here. MacArthur said, well, welcome here, but you aren't quite replacing Carl because Carl is on his way back from New York and he will be here soon. He knew everything about all of us all the time.

Q. When the end of World War II finally came, you were one of the very first photographers to set foot in Japan and you got such a prized position to shoot from at the surrender, it must have suddenly seemed that it had all been worthwhile, that the years of combat coverage had paid off, that your friendships with MacArthur and so many other American generals had helped get you to a position where you could take some of the most historic pictures of the twentieth century.

A. Yes, when I look at those pictures I made on the *Missouri* showing the war coming to its official end, I realize they are a consequence of my covering that war. But getting that prime position wasn't automatic. Shelley and I were living in a house on the waterfront of Manila when the electrifying news arrived that we had dropped the atomic bomb on Hiroshima and then a couple of days later on Nagasaki and that the Japanese were now asking if they could surrender. Everything was moving fast. All the press met one night in a great army tent to hear General Diller make an announcement about the plans to get us to Japan. Not much of an admirer of the press, Diller said a contingent of Allied correspondents would be sent in, and that meant everybody—New Zealanders, Australians, Americans, British, French, all of us who were Allies fighting the Japanese. He said there were only to be six of us in that contingent. That was the word from MacArthur. We can't handle the rest. So this time, Diller said, instead of me getting into trouble over who is picked, I am telling you I don't care who goes in, you choose who will represent you. And with that he walked out of the tent. So after all those years of fighting in the vast Pacific, it all came down to a concentrated battle in that tent. Correspondents were standing up on chairs shrieking, I have been covering this war for four years. No son of a bitch is going to keep me from going in to the surrender of Japan. The man from the *New York Times* got up and made a speech saying don't think of the *New York Times* as just a daily newspaper; we have a series of newspapers that use us; we are as important as the wire services. And then one correspondent got up and made the most absurd suggestion. He said, fellows, we've been in this war together —many of us since the beginning. And I move that if we can't all go into the surrender of Japan, none of us go in. Let's tell Diller none of us will go in. And somebody else, standing on a chair, followed quickly, who the hell ever heard of war reporters deciding that they wouldn't cover the surrender of the biggest war in history?

At that point I got the eye of a small handful of the war photographers, maybe six or seven of us, signaling to them to come out of the tent. We stood out in the darkness and I said look, those guys, the writers, don't care about us and we are not going to care about them. Let's all get together and thumb our way to Okinawa—that's where the jump-off is going to be. The hell with the writers. Let's get into Japan ourselves. So we all went to our little billets in various parts of Manila and met later at Nichols Field and got onto various aircraft.

In those days a war correspondent could just go up to a plane and say hey where are you going, I am with the AP or I am with *LIFE* magazine. That's the way we traveled. You always could find somebody who would take you. So we all flew to Okinawa.

I don't know what happened in that tent after we left, but within twenty-four hours airplanes were bringing writers in. And pretty soon we were all assembled on Okinawa. Then another battle began. The participants were not only the entire press corps in the Pacific, but the Allied press of the world as well, including scores and scores of people from the Pentagon and Washington who had been doing various desk jobs and now had come out for the kill, the end of the war. The numbers of war correspondents on Okinawa kept increasing. They had to put up extra mess tents to feed everybody. Then word came that we were going to leave the next day, and there was an increasing fight among the correspondents over who would be in the first plane. The first outfit going in was the Eleventh Airborne, which was commanded by General Joe Swing. The argument now centered around who would be with General Swing on that first plane. I must tell you, General Swing and I were very good friends from combat days. That was very important—to be known as a correspondent or a war photographer who was with them in combat. If a guy appeared and they didn't know him from combat, well, he was just another correspondent. But if they remembered that you were with them during the fighting, that you came through the same things they came through, they went out of their way to help you with whatever you needed.

We all went up that morning to General Swing's tent, most of us looking disheveled and unshaved—the war was coming to an end and we didn't give a damn. And then Joe Swing came out of his tent, freshly shaved, wearing starched field greens, his hat smartly tilted, a swagger stick in his hand and saying to us good morning gentlemen, well what can I do for you? And there was a moment of silence and then everybody's voice began at once and he held up his hand and said just a minute now, I can't understand a word you are saying. Is there anybody here who wants to explain what the trouble is, what your problem is. And somebody, I think it was a wire service man, spoke up and said, well General we want to be sure some of us are on that first plane with you and we want to speak up for that position. Swing looked around, he looked at all of us and he said well, you know one plane is not going to take all of you, and I think you know that since I command this division I will be in that plane and then he looked around and said I'll tell you, I will solve the problem. I will name the people whom I can carry in my plane. And he said, pointing at me, now I will begin with this little guy here. You know he's so small I can put him in my musette bag and I wouldn't even know he is there.

Yes, being in combat, knowing the generals, covering the war over a long time helped a lot.

After the Japanese surrender Mydans worked in Japan and then returned to the U.S. In 1946 one of his assignments took him to the Pacific atoll of Bikini to cover preparations for the H-bomb test. In 1947

Mydans became Time-Life bureau chief in Tokyo. In 1950–51 he covered the Korean War. Subsequent years found him on assignment in Britain, Switzerland, France, Germany, Egypt, Italy, Iran, Norway, Portugal, Nigeria. In 1959 he and Shelley and their two children took up residence in Moscow. While there, Francis Gary Powers and the U-2 were shot down and Mydans' pictures of the wreckage helped confirm it to the world. The 1960s found Mydans back in the Philippines with MacArthur and, among other places, in Hong Kong, Japan, Greenland, Samoa, Antigua, Tristan da Cunha, Yugoslavia, Bulgaria, Rumania, Easter Island. In 1968 he was in Vietnam, doing a story on refugees. Based again in Japan in 1969, Mydans covered stories all over the South Pacific. He returned to New York at the end of 1971. The year that followed was to be *LIFE*'s last as a weekly. "At 7:30 A.M. on December 8 (which is Pearl Harbor Day in the Philippines and my special 'day of infamy') *LIFE*'s picture editor telephoned me and said, 'There's to be a meeting at 10:30 and I think you would want to be there.' 'What's happening?' I asked, though I very well knew what was happening. He answered, 'I can't talk about it, Carl.'" Today, twelve years after the death of the weekly *LIFE*, with the magazine back as a monthly, Carl and Shelley live in Larchmont, New York. He still keeps his office in the Time-Life Building in New York City, he still takes assignments, he is still in love with photography, he still faces each new day with exhilaration and wonderment.

Q. During our talks, Carl, I asked you what photographers you admire most and you told me that among the photojournalists you most admire are David Douglas Duncan, Alfred Eisenstaedt, Gordon Parks, George Silk, Eugene Smith, Eddie Adams, and a few others. But Duncan was definitely number one on your list. Why?

A. Well, first because he is a good photographer. I've looked at his pictures for years, and he's got one of the best eyes I have ever seen. Next, he's a photojournalist of the first order. Remember there is a great deal of misunderstanding on what kind of a photographer is what. My years have been spent as a photojournalist, and a photojournalist is a storyteller—that is what I am, a storyteller. And David is a storyteller. I have looked at what he has done many times and admired him as a storyteller. He is next a compassionate man. And then there is another element that I measure him by, because it happens that my life has turned that way, and that is he's got a lot of courage. Now a lot of people won't measure a photographer by whether he's got a lot of courage—but I do, simply because I know something about the demands it makes.

Q. Courage. War. Danger. Bloodshed. At some point, Carl, you must have made a conscious decision to be involved in all that. You were thrown into that situation in Finland by an enterprising magazine groping for ways to get photographs of fighting. But you went back and back. You have almost been killed many times. You've been in Japanese prison camps for twenty-two months and after your release you were right back there again. With bridges being mined and blown up all around you and being shot at by Italians or Japanese or Koreans or Vietnamese. What was going on in your head?

A. Sometimes people have asked me but Carl why did you devote so much of your life to covering these terrible scenes, these disasters, these wars. And there is an important reason. When I began as a photojournalist I was interested in the history that was developing around me, whether it was the hundreds and hundreds of people I photographed who were the homeless, wandering along the roads during the days of the Farm Security Administration, or other pretty heart-rending scenes that I saw in those days.

Why did I pursue those scenes? Because they were evidence of one of the most important developments of my time, and I have been attracted all my life to important historical developments. Some were good, lots of them were not. And I had and still have a compulsion to record history. Remember, after *LIFE* was born, we went through years of war. Now it is true I could have done what some photojournalists did and in some way avoided war. But I have never avoided covering a development of our time because it threatened me. I do not think of myself as tough. That is your word, not mine. Determined is a much better description. It has never been too cold or too hot or too hard or too tiring for me to keep on going on a story worth telling. And war is one of those stories.

I want to make it clear it is not because I liked war. They were awful periods. I have often been in places where it was so terrible, where I was so frightened, where I would criticize myself for being there by saying what are you doing, why are you here. The answer always has been that what I am doing is important, and that's why I am here. I am making an historic record of a period of our times.

And somebody else might say gee, you can make an historic record of the paintings being offered to the Corcoran Gallery or something like that. But my interest is in recording active history being made. And one of the reasons why I am so interested in what happens to my negatives and my pictures is that I want those negatives and those pictures to be lasting. Long after I am gone I want people to be able to see through my eyes and know what happened.

I want to say something else. Just as I said a few minutes ago that there were terrible times and I would say my God why, there were other times that were not terrible, that were telling and human and simple and moving, and I think of them more often than the terrible times. In Italy, for instance, I was with an infantry outfit. There was a battle for one of the Italian towns and it was a bloodbath. It was late in the day and I had been working four, five days in the field with only enough time to ship my film and get back with another outfit. The outfit I was with was moving up. And, as I have said, I always was more scared when the day was coming to an end.

I was walking with an infantry outfit along a road, lugging—always lugging my own stuff—there were no vehicles among these infantrymen. Then, I heard a jeep behind me. It was coming down the middle of the road, and I just continued walking. When the jeep got alongside me and stopped I looked up and I saw there was a colonel sitting in it. He said can I give you a lift, and I said well I am with this outfit and I want to stay with them for the night. He said, it is my outfit, why don't you come on up here with me and let me take you part way.

So I climbed in the jeep with him and we got talking about the war and covering the war. Then he was going off in another direction and as I was getting out of the jeep, he said well I want to thank you. And I said for what? He said I want to thank you for being here with my outfit. Not many people know it, but these kids are all out here doing something important and some of them are getting hurt doing it. They like to think that somebody is out here with them and is telling the folks back home.

That's what I was doing—telling the folks back home.

This book is made up entirely of black-and-white photographs in an age when color has increasingly captured the interest of photographers. Some viewers see little difference between the two, except that one is brighter than the other. But there is a dimension in black-and-white that produces a profoundly different art form.

The artistry of printing is done after the picture has been made and the negative processed. It is a creation in semidarkness by skilled photo-printers who manipulate light and chemistry in a remarkable modern alchemy. There are fewer and fewer of these photo-printers left, but a team of the very best continues to be nurtured in the Time & Life photo labs, and it is they who printed the pictures in this book. To them and to their two master-printer supervisors, Carmine Ercolano and John Downey, my appreciation and thanks.

PREWAR U.S.A.

Daughter of migrant workers near Raymondville, Texas, 1937.

(Right) *Fifty-four-year-old construction engineer Maurice J. Shannon, unemployed because of the Depression, looks for a job on Hollywood's Sunset Boulevard, July 1939.*

(Far right) *A pioneer organizer of the Office Workers' Union exhorts a crowd of sympathizers at a noontime rally at Wall and Broad streets in New York City in 1936.*

(Below) *Political banners for the election of 1936 span a street in Hardwick, Vermont. Vermont was one of only two states to vote against Roosevelt in his landslide over Landon. (Farm Security Administration photograph)*

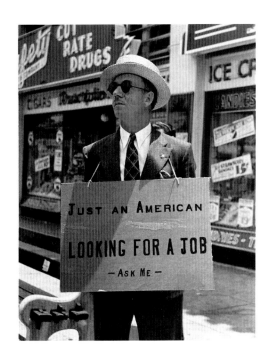

(Top) *A view of the nation's Capitol through a nearby slum area, 1935. (FSA)*

(Above) *Children play in the slums behind the Capitol, Washington, D.C. (FSA)*

(Right) *In the depths of the Great Depression, one quarter of the entire American work force was unemployed. In Chicago the number was nearly half. Here one of their number sits bowed under the spring sun on Michigan Avenue, 1936.*

A migratory worker who has lost his farm stares at the past, Raymondville, Texas.

(Opposite) *A boy looks at the future in the oil boom town of Freer, Texas, 1937.*

(Opposite top) *South Street on New York's waterfront, in Depression years, 1935.*

(Opposite bottom) *"Chain gang" of New York Stock Exchange officers carries traded securities each day to banks and brokerage houses, 1937.*

(Above top) *Horse traders talking business, Albany, Vermont, 1936. (FSA)*

(Above) *The daily morning gathering at City Hall, Batesville, Arkansas, 1936. (FSA)*

Schoolyard in Scottsboro, Alabama, 1936. (FSA)

Multigrade school in Scottsboro. (FSA)

Young men of the Civilian Conservation Corps clear the land in Prince Georges County, Maryland, 1936. (FSA)

An amateur barber works on Fulton Pier, East River, New York City, 1936.

Migrant workers like this man whom I found living with his family by the side of the road near Raymondville, Texas, in 1937, were called brush-hogs.

(Opposite) *Transient cotton choppers in Crittenden County, Arkansas, in 1936, on the road to find a better-paying plantation. "Damned if we'll work for what they pay folks hereabouts," they told me. (FSA)*

Father and son wear their hats to pose in their
Cincinnati tenement, 1936. (FSA)

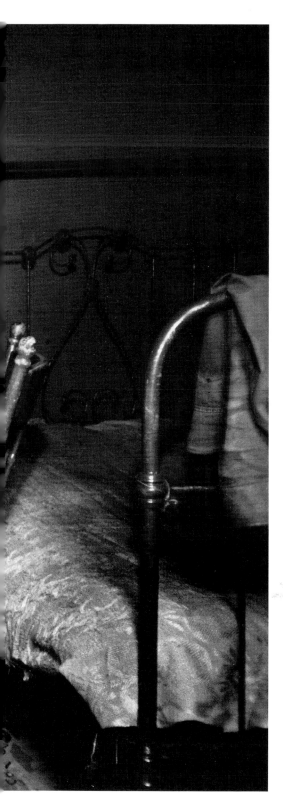

A model displays an evening dress for customers at Neiman-Marcus department store, Dallas, Texas, 1938.

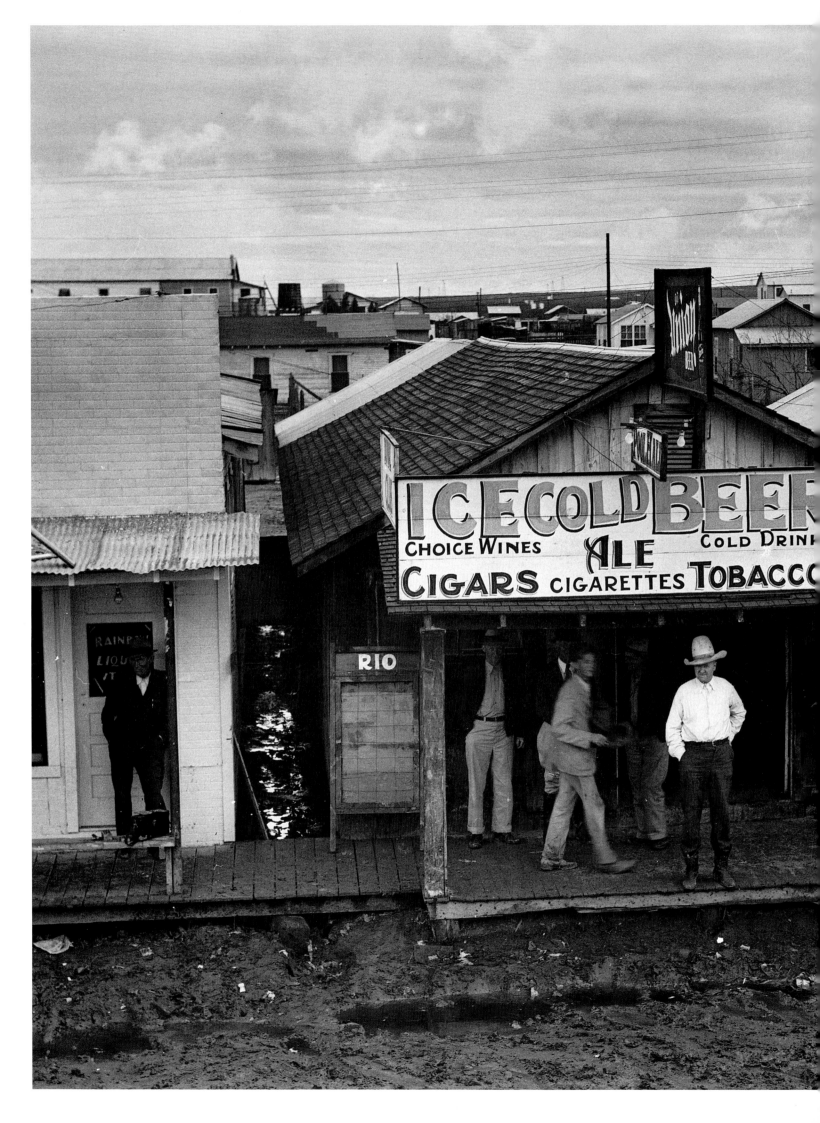

Loungers hang around the Duval Club lunchroom
in Freer, Texas, 1937

A thousand whiteface cattle entering Eagle Pass, Texas, after a hundred-mile drive from Cohuila, Mexico, 1937.

A whiteface steer charging, Texas, 1937. A photographer often concentrates so intently on what he is seeing that he is not aware of danger, and I was not frightened until I saw this picture.

A general store in the Big Bend country, at Terlingua, Texas, 1937.

Main street in the oil boom town of Freer, Texas, 1937.

(Above) *Police chief of an oil boom town exemplifies the Texas lawman, 1937.*

Texas cowboy of the Old West with his trusty cowpony predate the Marlboro Man, 1938.

Roustabouts in Freer, Texas, take time off from their jobs, 1937.

Camp follower in the wide-open town of Freer.

Sandhogs working under the East River in New York City, 1939.

(Opposite) *A sandhog tests a cast-iron plate in the frame of a tunnel being constructed under the East River in New York City. A sandhog is a laborer who works in compressed air.*

(Above) *A hundred feet below the East River in New York City, a sandhog calls out the number of inches of the "shove" as the shield is pushed forward against rock, muck, and the great pressure of river water.*

(Left) *In a running game of "21" sandhogs gamble with their wages while waiting to go to work below the river.*

(Opposite) *Sandhogs wait for their work shift during the building of the East River tunnel in New York City.*

DEFEAT IN EUROPE AND ASIA

*A London news vendor defies the enemy during the first fright-
ening months of World War II. The Nazis invaded Poland in
September 1939 and I was sent to cover the war. In England the
British dug trenches in the parks, sandbagged their buildings,
blacked out their windows, carried gas masks in paper boxes
—and waited.*

Frightened Russian prisoners and frozen Russian dead testify to the agonies of the Russo-Finnish War of 1939. While the French and Germans watched each other across the Maginot Line the Russians invaded Finland, and in that short, bitter conflict in the sub-zero cold north of the Arctic Circle I photographed my first battlefields and witnessed for the first time man's cruel violence to man.

Mussolini among his sycophants in Parliament put on the best show of all, 1940.

(Right) LIFE captioned this picture of Mussolini strutting before the Victor Emmanuel Monument in Rome in 1940 "The Elderly Butcher Boy of Fascism Steps Out," and the entire bureaus of Time and LIFE were expelled from Italy.

Fascist Italy in 1940 had such a gloss of showmanship that a photographer could easily forget the bullying politics, the jails, and the death chambers.

In Fascist Italy art is eternal, humanity passing.

(Opposite) *A Fascist dignitary in Rome struts beneath a bronze image of Romulus and Remus, the city's legendary founders.*

(Above) *A bored Florentine gentleman ignores the plight of a Sabine woman in Giovanni da Bologna's famous sculpture.*

(Above) *"Each war begins where the last one left off." French soldiers in May 1940 could be mistaken for the poilus of 1914 as they straggle past a shelled village near Verdun after the German breakthrough at Sedan.*

(Top, left and right) *As the Germans converge on Paris, French citizens flee south.*

(Opposite) *Officers of a French tank brigade take their mess alfresco in a forest near Verdun after the German breakthrough.*

(Opposite) *In China's Central Air-raid Control Center, deep in a secret cave in Chungking in 1941, warnings of approaching planes come in from spotters in Japanese territory. In the city, sirens sound and warning lanterns are run up poles.*

(Above) *Chungking under Japanese bombing, June 1941.*

(Above) *The agony of China shows in the face of this refugee from one of the prosperous cities now occupied by the Japanese, 1941.*

(Opposite top) *Chair carriers like beasts of burden carry travelers and their goods up the steep steps from the Kialing River in Chungking, 1941.*

(Opposite bottom) *Conscripts of the Chinese Nationalist Army walk through Chungking on a labor detail. The eyes of the man in the foreground have haunted me ever since I saw them through the viewfinder.*

From an ancient fort beside the Yellow River in Tungkuan, Nationalist soldiers fire at the Japanese dug in across the river in the Sino-Japanese War, 1941.

(Left) *A trench dug in the soft loess earth beside the Yellow River supplants the railroad that has been shelled by the Japanese.*

(Above top) *Exhausted Chinese laborers sleep in a teahouse in Chungking.*

(Above middle) *"Foreign devils," especially with cameras, are objects of suspicion to Chinese villagers in Szechuan.*

(Above) *The life of a ricksha puller is short.*

(Right) *When there is food, Chinese laborers rest and eat beside the streets where they work.*

Chopsticks are ubiquitous in China. Farm people in the villages use wooden ones; in Chungking, Generalissimo Chiang Kai-shek and Madame Chiang use ivory.

Four generations of the prosperous farming family of Fang Ta-chi on the rich plain of central Szechuan pose for my camera in front of the ancestral room in their farmhouse in 1941.

They are, from left to right, top row: Third Son of First Son; First Son of First Son; First Son of Second Son; Sixth Son; First Son; Second Son; First Son of Seventh Son with his infant second son in his arms; Fourth Son of First Son; First Son of Sixth Son. Seated are: Wife of Third Son of First Son; Wife of Sixth Son; seventy-five-year-old Grandfather Fang; Wife of Second Son holding her third daughter; Third Wife of First Son; Second Wife of First Son of First Son. In front row are some of the children.

Others of the family refuse to have their pictures taken, fearing that when their image is taken away on film their souls will follow.

The wooden-paddled waterwheel that raises water from a lower to a higher paddy field is manned by sons of the family who own the farm.

(Opposite) The volunteer fire brigade in the market village of Lung Chuan-I, in central Szechuan, spontaneously took this pose when I asked if I could photograph them, 1941.

(Above) *A teahouse in Lung Chuan-I presents a scene so full of life and movement, diversity of human forms and faces, that a photographer is entranced, 1941.*

(Left) *Straw hats, woven by local farm women, are a special product of the region.*

(Opposite) *The main street of the prosperous village (population about 10,000) is busy day and night.*

(Above) *An opium smoker holds his government permit as a British officer approaches in an opium den in Singapore in 1941.*

(Opposite top) *Opium smokers are mostly ricksha pullers and day laborers who need the drug to dull the pain of their lives. The opium has been manufactured by the local British government and is sold to licensed addicts.*

(Opposite bottom) *Sleep and oblivion reward the opium smoker.*

A Sikh officer in the Indian Army under British command in Singapore, 1941.

(Opposite) *A Chinese tin worker in a British-owned mine in Malaya, 1941.*

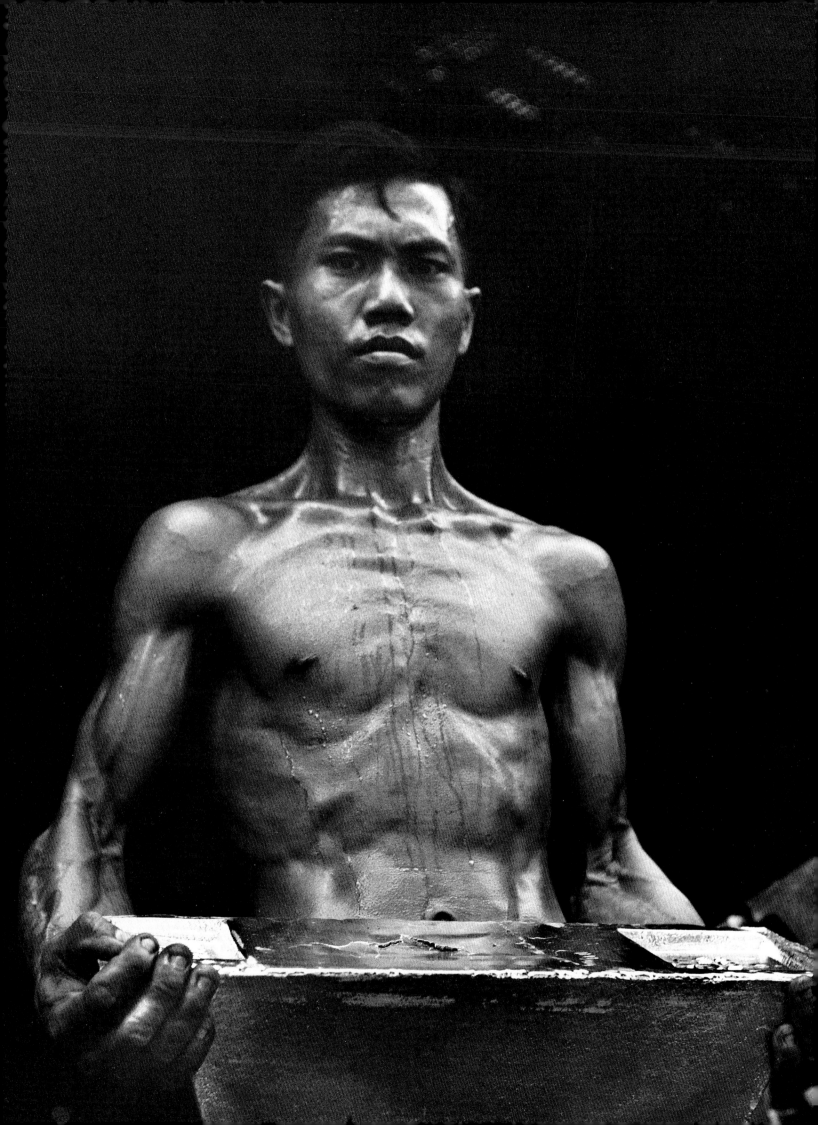

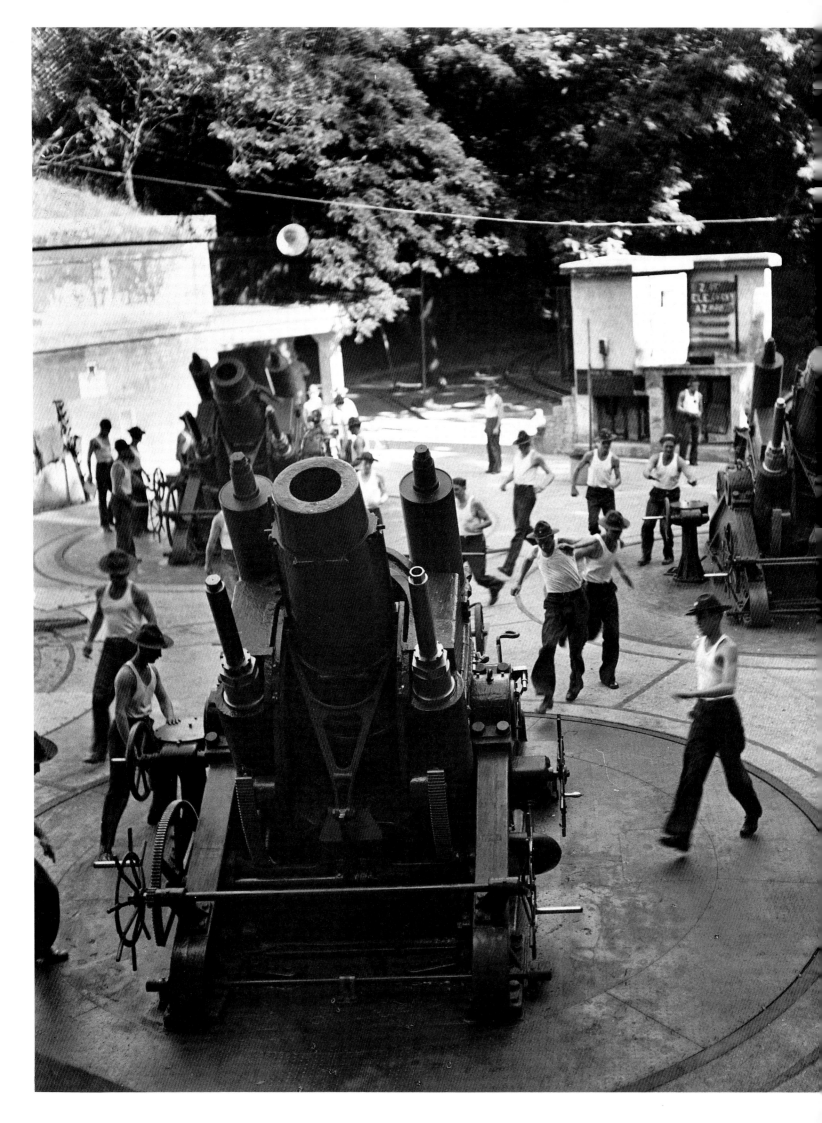

(Above) *American fighter and bomber pilots take shelter in a shallow trench at Clark Field in the Philippines after Japanese air attacks destroyed their planes on the ground on the first day of the war. Some of these pilots, and many others, got out to fly again; some fought and died as infantry soldiers on Bataan and Corregidor; some died in Japanese prison camps.*

(Left) *American marines drill with mortars on the fortress island of Corregidor in Manila Bay just before Pearl Harbor. Corregidor's big guns proved useless when the Japanese bombed and shelled them, 1941.*

(Right) *Philippine Scouts attached to American forces in Manila on patrol in the canebrake on Luzon only a few days before the Japanese strike in December 1941.*

VICTORY IN EUROPE AND ASIA

*Units of the American Third Division enter a newly
liberated village in the south of France, August 1944.*

Mother and child in an Italian refugee camp, Cesano, Italy. The father was taken by the Germans when they retreated, 1944.

(Opposite) *A German prisoner is taken in the fighting south of Rome, May 1944.*

*Fascist Police Chief Pietro Caruso, Questore of Rome, sits
before a firing squad after the liberation of Rome, 1944.*

*Captured Germans, during the battle for Rome, 1944,
await shipment to prison enclosure.*

German dead on the road to Rome, 1944.

(Opposite) *The abbey of Monte Cassino, Italy, after Allied bombing in the spring of 1944.*

(Above) *Two German soldiers are captured near Saint-Tropez in the liberation of southern France.*

(Opposite above) *Units of the American Third Division enter a newly liberated village in the south of France, August 1944.*

(Opposite below) *A file of surrendering German soldiers taken by the French is marched through a village.*

A French Maquis surfaces in Grenoble after the liberation.

(Opposite above and below) *French women accused of sleeping with Germans during the occupation are shaved by vindictive neighbors in a village near Marseilles, August 1944.*

(Above) *A young Frenchman, convicted of collaboration with the Germans, is tied to a stake in Grenoble in September 1944.*

(Opposite above) *Six Frenchmen, convicted of collaboration, are executed by a firing squad in Grenoble.*

(Opposite below) *The coup de grâce is given to young collaborators.*

General Douglas MacArthur wades ashore at Lingayen Gulf in Luzon, the Philippines, on January 9, 1945.

(Above) *General MacArthur fords a river in a jeep on the race south to the battle of Manila, January 1945.*

(Opposite) *General MacArthur visits the battlefield on Bataan in March.*

(Top left) *Intermuros, the old walled city of Manila, under shelling by the Americans, January 1945.*

(Middle left) *G.I.s under fire carry a wounded soldier during the fighting in Manila.*

(Left) *A Catholic chaplain holds mass outside a ruined church in Manila.*

(Upper right) *American troops and Filipino guerrillas join in the battle against the Japanese on the road to Manila.*

Wounded Filipina women are carried to a field hospital in a makeshift ambulance during the fight for Manila.

The Legislative Building in Manila after the shelling in January 1945.

(Opposite) *Death and devastation in the streets of Manila after the battle of January–February 1945.*

(Above) *Lee Rogers and John Todd lost 131 pounds between them during their four years in Santo Tomas, and both suffered from beriberi. I shared a room with them and thirty-five other men before I was transferred to China and eventually repatriated.*

(Opposite above) *A family that survived intact four years of internment in the civilian prison camp of Santo Tomas, Manila. Children were always fed first.*

(Opposite below) *American civilian P.O.W. in the same camp.*

(Top) *Mamoru Shigemitsu and General Yoshijiro Umezu stand ready to sign surrender papers on the deck of the U.S.S.* Missouri. *Ex-Foreign Minister Shigemitsu lost a leg to Korean terrorists and needs the support of a cane.*

(Above) *At the Kurihama Naval Base, the Japanese naval commander surrenders his sword to an American marine officer, September 1945. Never again in a world of changing warfare will such a scene of chivalry take place.*

The Japanese surrender on board the U.S.S. Missouri *in Tokyo Bay on September 2, 1945. General Yoshijiro Umezu signs the surrender document while General MacArthur looks on.*

Wary enemies pass on the road to Yokohama. Japanese soldiers, still armed, are deployed along the route of the conqueror. Their backs are turned as a sign of respect, 1945.

(Opposite) Americans and Japanese astonish each other. The first jeep to drive from Atsugi airfield, where the first contingent of Americans landed, into Yokohama encounters a farmer with his household on his cart.

AFTERMATH

North Korean soldiers taken by U.S. Marines during the fighting for Yong Dong in 1950 are marched to the rear.

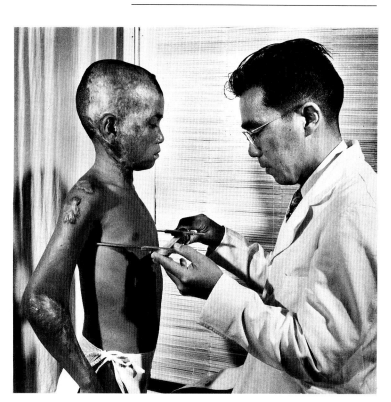

(Above top) *A victim of the Hiroshima bombing, four years after the blast, is measured in a Japanese-American medical study of the effects of nuclear contamination.*

(Above bottom) *Three survivors of the atomic bomb sit under a blasted tree in a graveyard in Hiroshima, 1947.*

(Opposite) *Two years after the Hiroshima bombing, a woman draws water in the midst of the rubble, 1947.*

Relief rice for starving Japan is unloaded from a ship in Kobe Harbor during the American occupation.

(Top) *General Jiro Minami is brought from Sugamo Prison in Tokyo to the War Crimes Tribunal by American military guards, 1948. He was found guilty, sentenced to life imprisonment, and paroled in 1954.*

(Above) *General Minami, a defendant in the major war crimes trials in Tokyo.*

(Opposite) *General Kingoro Hashimoto at the end of his long trial for war crimes in 1948. In these pictures he is praying instants before the verdict is given, listening to the verdict, and being crushed by it. He received a life sentence and was paroled in 1955.*

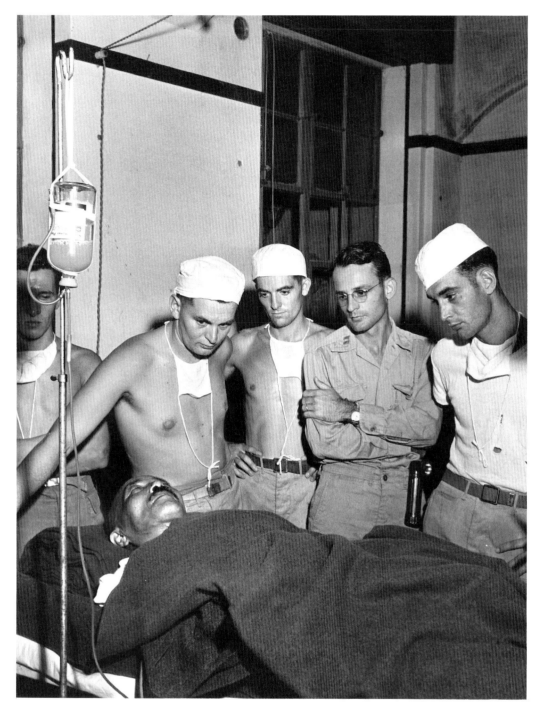

General and former Prime Minister Hideki Tojo re-
ceives blood from an American Army unit and has
just regained consciousness after he botched a
suicide attempt in 1945. When Tojo saw General
Robert Eichelberger standing at his bedside, Tojo
told him he was sorry for all the trouble he was
causing. Eichelberger said to the interpreter, "Ask
him if he means the trouble tonight, or the last four
years?"

General Tojo at his war crimes trial in Tokyo. After the occupation forces saved his life in 1945 its Military Tribunal found him guilty and hanged him in 1948. (In front of him are his lawyers and a Russian general of the Tribunal.)

The newly created "Japanese Police Force" maneuvers in the snow in Hokkaido. The American-inspired Japanese Constitution renounced war, but in 1951, at the urging of the United States, Japan began building an army.

(Above) *A major earthquake struck Fukui on the west coast of Honshu in 1948. I had just arrived in the city and was at the epicenter taking pictures within instants of the disaster. Here, the Hiwa department store begins to crumble as I view it through my camera.*

(Above right) *Many people were trapped in their burning homes, but some lucky ones escaped with a few possessions.*

(Below right) *A man carrying his dead wife whispered "too late" so his son, holding his mother's hand, won't hear.*

(Opposite) *As fire raced through the ruins, survivors fled along streets that cracked open under their feet.*

Chiang Kai-shek's forces in full retreat wind through the streets
of Nanking in 1949, as the Communists envelop the Chinese
capital.

(Opposite, above and below) *Chinese Nationalist forces on the
run from the Communists during the civil war, 1949, bivouac in
the wheatlands near Pengpu, Anhwei province.*

Out in the barren wheatlands of Anhwei a burial takes place. This is a poor family who can afford only a crude unfinished coffin and one professional mourner draped in white.

(Opposite) *After the war between the Nationalists and the Communists passed through a village near Pengpu, I found only this old woman mourning in the ruins.*

(Opposite) *In Indochina in 1950, a French army outpost overlooks a Viet Minh sanctuary in the sawtooth mountains of China just ahead.*

(Above) *The ruins of French prosperity stand empty on this abandoned rubber estate in French Indochina during the war with the Viet Minh.*

A Turkish soldier of the United Nations forces in the Korean War stands watch in the frosty dawn.

(Opposite) A Korean woman with her child, fleeing from the fighting around Seoul during the winter of 1951, drinks from the frozen Han River.

(Top) *Korean women suspected of Communist sympathies are seized by South Korean soldiers.*

(Opposite) *After the short-lived but bloody Communist uprising at Yosu in 1948, a family finds its dead.*

(Above) *Mutinous soldiers of the South Korean army taken prisoner after the aborted uprising are trucked to their court-martial trials.*

(Above from top to bottom)

G.I.s shelter under their ponchos during the Korean War.

The first American killed in the Korean War is surrounded by his comrades.

U.S. Marines pass a burning Korean village in the winter rain.

General Douglas MacArthur with army, marine, navy, and air force commanders watches the assault landing at Inchon, Korea, in 1951—one of the most daring amphibious operations in the history of war.

*Korean civilians in a gully near Taejon were massacred by
retreating North Korean forces in 1950.*

(Opposite) *North Korean soldiers taken by U.S. Marines during
the fighting for Yong Dong in 1950 are marched to the rear.*

A medic in the Turkish Brigade of the United Nations forces gives aid to a burned Korean woman at the edge of the battlefield.

(Opposite) *A Korean mother carrying her baby and her worldly goods flees the fighting around Seoul in the winter attack on the Korean capital in 1951.*

POSTWAR

Frau Mai scrapes the pot to feed her husband and three boys, in 1954.

Good times in a London pub.

(Top) *The Queen, Queen Mother, and Princess Royal prepare for a wedding reception at St. James's Palace, London.*

(Above) *The Queen's Messenger leaves Buckingham Palace with dispatches for the Foreign Office.*

(Left) *Princess Margaret arrives in London to a deferential greeting.*

The eccentric rector of Warleggan, the Reverend Frederick W. Bensham, 83, glories in his eccentricity. He died alone and I was one of only three people at his funeral in 1953.

(Opposite) *At Warleggan Church in Cornwall, England, the rector leads a lonely life, having quarreled with his parish.*

(Above left) *In Swansea, Wales, the fog comes in over the chimney pots.*

(Left) *British coal miner Dixen Bell takes a break three hundred feet down in the mine.*

(Above) *In a colliery club in Yorkshire, miners relax with a pint.*

(Right) *Down in the mines in 1952, British coal miners work eighteen-inch narrow seams.*

Coal miner, Durham, England, 1952.

(Opposite) *Coal miner's daughter, Yorkshire, 1952.*

A plaza in the little town of Alaejos, Spain, 1953.

(Opposite) *Feluccas on the Nile, Egypt, 1953.*

Potato planting in Limburg, Germany, 1954.

(Above) *Emma Mai, of Ansbach, Bavaria, gathers faggots in the forest near her home during the pinched years of postwar Germany.*

(Above right) *Fredi Mai prepares for his First Communion.*

(Right) *The Mai family shoes wear out despite frequent patching, but the cost of new shoes is prohibitive in Germany in 1954.*

(Opposite) *Frau Mai does the family laundry in her courtyard.*

A Russian officer kisses the flag at a demobilization ceremony in Minsk, U.S.S.R.

(Opposite) *The Kremlin and Spassky Tower, Moscow, under a full moon.*

(Top) *Women sweep the pavement of Manège Square while units of the Soviet Red Army march toward Red Square.*

(Above) *Nikita Khrushchev on his visit to the U.S., 1959.*

(Opposite) *Military march-past in 1960 in Red Square, Moscow, on the forty-second anniversary of the October Revolution.*

A Polynesian family in American Samoa.

(Opposite) *A Micronesian mother and son on Ulithi in the Caroline Islands.*

Vietnamese refugee made homeless by the Tet offensive in Saigon, 1968.

(Opposite) *A Vietnamese grandmother and child during the Tet offensive.*

(Opposite) *American tourists in American Samoa.*

(Above) *Senior citizens still dance with vigor in an American home for the elderly.*

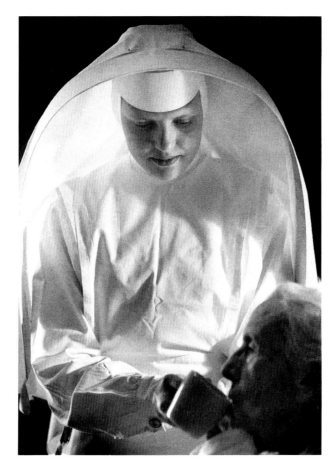

Sister Maureen Therese feeds Mamie Lucas, 88, in the Carroll Manor home for the aged, near Washington, D.C.

(Opposite) *Aged mental patients in a state hospital.*

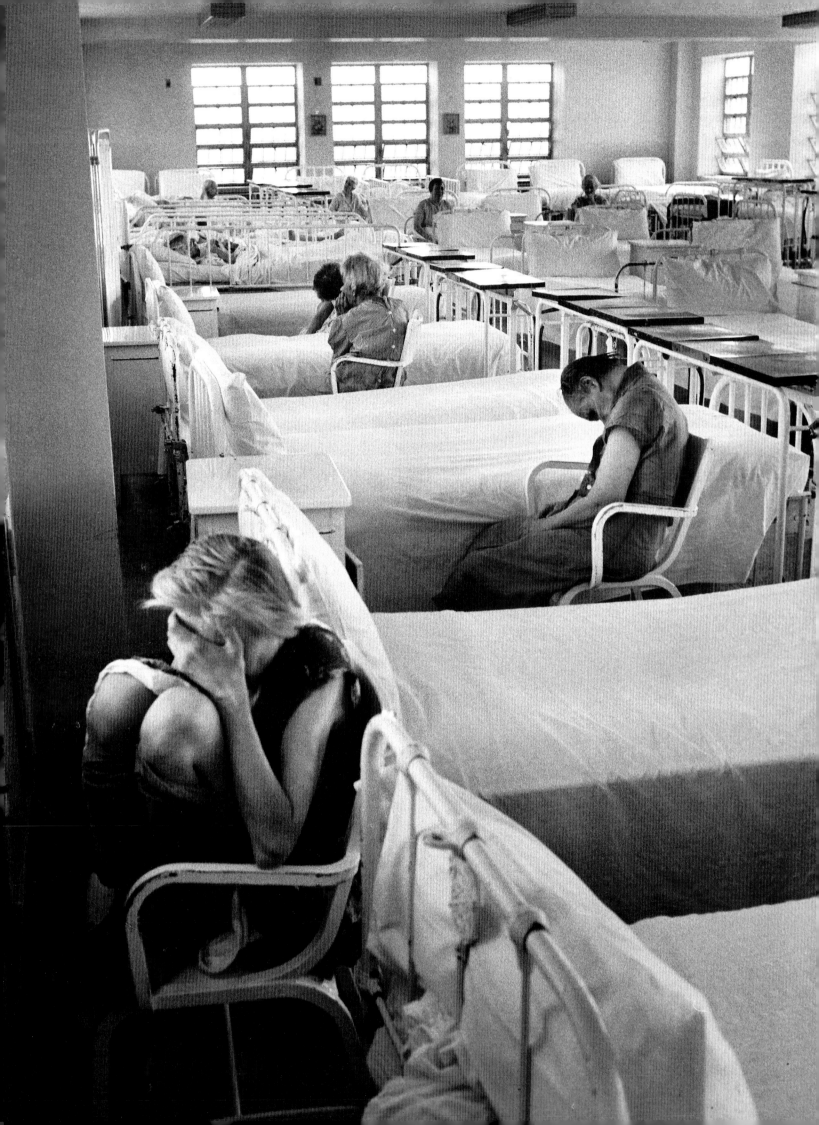

(Opposite) *On the Nixon campaign trail in 1956.*   (Above) *Senator Joe McCarthy has his picture taken in 1951.*

Senator John F. Kennedy campaigning with his wife in Boston, 1958.

Headlines, November 22, 1963, on a commuter train to Stamford, Connecticut.

PERSONALITIES

Kuo Tung, a coffin maker of Lanchow, China, was 130 years old in 1941.

India's first president, Pandit Jawaharlal Nehru, 1956.

Indira Gandhi in Canada, 1956.

General Hideki Tojo at his war crimes trial, 1947.

(Opposite) *General Douglas MacArthur in his plane, the* Bataan, *during the Korean War.*

General Sadao Araki, War Minister of Japan during his trial for war crimes.

(Above) *Leonard Bernstein with the New York Philharmonic Orchestra in Moscow, 1959.*

(Opposite) *Ezra Pound, poet, in Milan, Italy, 1940.*

Fascist Propaganda Minister of Rome Pavolini under a portrait of Mussolini, Italy, 1940.

(Opposite) *Eamon De Valera, President of Ireland, under a plaque of the martyred patriot Michael Collins.*

Secretary of State John Foster Dulles at the United Nations, 1958.

Dr. Mohammed Mossadegh, premier of Iran, at his trial in Teheran, 1953.

(Opposite) *Nikita Khrushchev denouncing President Eisenhower, Moscow, 1960, after the U-2 was shot down.*

Nobel Prize Laureate William Faulkner at West Point, 1962.

Walter Lippmann, journalist, sage, and political advisor, in his Washington home, 1964.

(Opposite) *German novelist Thomas Mann in his home at Princeton, New Jersey, 1939.*

Vice-President John Nance Garner in his office in the Capitol, Washington, D.C., 1939.

(Opposite) *Senators Harry S Truman and Burton K. Wheeler at the Capitol in 1939.*

Bobby Fischer, chess champion, in New York, 1962.

(Opposite) *Charles Lindbergh, aviation pioneer, environmentalist, and defender of primitive peoples, in the Philippines, 1970.*

(Top) *Carole Lombard and Clark Gable at a movie preview,*
Hollywood, 1936.

(Above) *Gertrude Stein and Alice B. Toklas with "Basket"*
at their home in southern France at the time of their liberation,
September 1944.

(Opposite) *Vladimir Nabokov, novelist and lepidopterist,*
in Ithaca, New York, in 1958.

Henry Kissinger, Professor of International Studies, at Harvard in 1958.

(Opposite) *Prime Minister Winston Churchill at Biggleswade, England, 1955.*